Advanced Social Work Practice

ADVANCED SOCIAL WORK PRACTICE

An Integrative, Multilevel Approach

JOAN DWORKIN, PH.D.

Professor, Division of Social Work
California State University, Sacramento

Boston   New York   San Francisco
Mexico City   Montreal   Toronto   London   Madrid   Munich   Paris
Hong Kong   Singapore   Tokyo   Cape Town   Sydney

Vice President/Editor-in-Chief: *Karen Hanson*
Series Editor: *Patricia Quinlin*
Senior Series Editorial Assistant: *Annemarie Kennedy*
Marketing Manager: *Taryn Wahlquist*
Electronic Composition: *Karen Mason*
Manufacturing Buyer: *Joanne Sweeney*
Cover Designer: *Joel Gendron*

For related titles and support materials, visit our online catalog at www.ablongman.com

ISBN: 0-205-37827-7

Printed in the United States of America

10 9 8 7 6 5 4 3 2   08 07 06 05

This book is dedicated to my family, who each in their own way has worked on multiple levels to make this world a better place for all of us: Jerry, my husband, a philosopher who provides ethical insights on some of the most challenging worldwide social issues; and my daughters, Lisa (Niquie), a clinical psychologist who helps people overcome critical and sometimes severe and unrelenting psychological challenges, and Julie, a policy advocate working in the persistent struggle to end homelessness.

CONTENTS

PREFACE

The case studies in this collection are specifically designed to provide learning opportunities, using problem-based learning and case scenarios, for advanced Masters of Social Work students. Using this book, students will gain skill in an integrated approach to social work practice at multiple levels.

Social work practice is organized around a variety of systems, which organize themselves around strata that range from "micro" to "macro" units of attention (Tropman and Richards-Schuster, 2000, p. 66). These levels include work with individuals, families, groups, organizations, communities, and social policies. The perspective of this book is that students must understand the close relationship between their clinical work, which is client-focused, and working for social justice, which most frequently is population-focused, to fully address the concerns and problems of the people they work with and to be able to act on them simultaneously. In order to bridge what has been an erroneous dichotomy, and given the myriad demands of today's workplace, graduate students must be prepared to be versatile practitioners.

The profile of current social work graduate students includes a large cohort of mature workers already experienced in the social services. They may be quite adept at their practice, yet to become more versatile are attending school to increase their knowledge base, to learn about theories that inform their work, and to be exposed to new ideas. Self-guided learning is an effective strategy for adult education. Young students with little or no experience may bring fresh insights and raise provocative questions. The use of case studies in small groups, using self-guided activities and shared learning, is very appropriate for both of these groups.

Another premise on which this book is based is that both students and faculty can enter a teaching/learning partnership based on a common understanding of the educational approach used. Therefore, Chapter 1 is designed to introduce both groups to the problem-based case study method. Chapter 8 provides further reflections on this method, discusses its future, and provides some research on using case studies.

The case studies in this book were collected from actual social service programs or organizations. Social work educators, students, faculty, and practitioners contributed case scenarios. They used a storytelling or oral history approach. For cases relayed to us orally, we reworked them into case vignettes to ensure confidentiality and to reflect the goal of teaching an integrated approach to practice at an advanced level. Contributors who submitted written case scenarios are credited for their cases. Cases have been kept as close to the original as possible to reflect the variety of perspectives and styles of contributors.

I have provided introductory material, learning objectives, and case activities to make each case study a more complete learning tool. Case-related activities are intentionally varied and include application of theory, critical analysis, written work, role-play, small group discussion, library research, oral argument, group problem solving, data collection in the community, program development, and social action. Students and instructors can select tasks from the variety of activities provided for each case that will provide desired learning opportunities.

Each scenario has been designed so that students can study and apply at least two levels of intervention to the case. Cases in most instances do not provide an intervention strategy but rather are constructed so that students must develop their own. Students are able to move from "case" to "cause" and then back again. In this collection, a case study may be entered at any intervention level and then studied from multiple vantage points. If the starting point is the client, the student learns to extrapolate the issues that may require intervention at another level, perhaps organization or community, which would address the population in which the client is a member. Conversely, if the case refers to an organization or community problem, the students can infer the impact on clients or families.

Frequently, students interpret referral of clients to a community-based organization as community intervention. In this book, community intervention means intervention "with" the community rather than "in" the community or referral to a community resource. Students who wish to pursue a specific topic further are encouraged to study the Suggested Readings included after each case. As a further aid for students, the Glossary at the end of the text contains definitions of many common terms students are likely to encounter in their social work studies.

ACKNOWLEDGMENTS

I wish to express my great appreciation to Scott Weber, an MSW student, who assisted me in the initial phases of compiling case studies for the case study manual on which this book is based. He assisted in all aspects of the development of the case study manual, including collection of case material from faculty, field instructors, and students; development of learning objectives; design of study questions; and transcribing, rewriting, and editing of cases. As a student participating in the Advanced Practice course during the preparation of the manual, Scott was able to provide a student's perspective and to articulate student learning needs as he perceived them from his peers.

I would like to thank the following faculty, field instructors, practitioners, and students who contributed to this case study manual or tested it in their classrooms: Tania Alameda-Lawson, Robin Carter, Roger Coe, Jennifer Cooreman, Angie Del Nero, Dave Demetral, Wynne DuBray, Janice Gagerman, Chuck Gatten, Juan Hernandez, Judy Ness, David Nylund, Candelaria Perez-Davidson, Arline

Prigoff, Julia Sak, Bev Short, Stephen Sikes, Judy Statsinger, Ben Tadakoro, Scott Weber, Brian Wong, and Patricia Wyrick.

I also wish to acknowledge the influence of my deceased colleague, Jerry Sachs of Smith College, whose work with Fred Newdom on the integration of clinical work and the fight for social justice was always at the forefront of my mind as I wrote this book.

Finally, I want to express my gratitude to California State University at Sacramento for granting me Pedagogy Enhancement Awards in two successive years, which helped to provide the resources to work on this project.

Advanced Social Work Practice

CHAPTER ONE

PROBLEM-BASED LEARNING AND THE CASE STUDY METHOD

AN INTEGRATED APPROACH

Historically, the case study has been one of the primary methods used in teaching social work practice. Devore and Schlesinger (1996) provide a comprehensive review of the use of the case study method for professional education. Typically, a "case" will focus on an individual, family, group, community, or perhaps a policy issue. Where multiple interventions are addressed, they are frequently taught sequentially from cases constructed to focus on a particular level or may emerge from a "micro-" focused case that then lends itself to advocacy, or possibly program development. The integrated approach to teaching and learning about multiple levels of social work intervention in this book cuts across fields of practice and methods. A fundamental change at the advanced level is the strengthening and reinforcing of the dual commitment of social work to both private and social justice concerns (Landon and Feit, 1999). The limited research that has been done on student attention to the dual perspective in social work indicates that students will tend to focus on "private issues" unless prompted (Nurius and Gibson, 1994, cited in Kemp, 1995, p. 187).

Therefore, a major challenge for social work educators is how to make a cognitive shift to an integrated approach, not only to transform their own thinking about cases but also that of their students. A review of several existing case texts (Kirst-Ashman and Hull, 1999; Rivas & Hull, 1996; and LeCroy, 1999, are examples of collections of cases that are widely used as texts) reveal that they do not sufficiently focus on guiding students toward a multifaceted approach to each case, which would direct students to move back and forth from "case" to "cause."

THE CASE FOR THE CASE STUDY METHOD

The Harvard Business School was using case studies at the turn of the century. Various businesses would contribute short scenarios to stimulate students to engage in problem solving of real cases with which they were struggling. Cases evolved from concise problems to more complex situations that include multiple factors (Barnes, Christensen, and Hansen, 1994, p. 44; McNair, 1954). After World War II, changes in the curriculum geared to a more administrative focus furthered support for the method. The method was not only seen as a way to engage students in dealing with business problems but was also considered beneficial to faculty, who would continuously be in touch with developments in the field as they produced new case material for their students. The case method currently is supported schoolwide. Classrooms are designed to promote maximum interaction between teachers and students and to foster student-to-student interaction (p. 42). While the case method is designed for use in small discussion groups averaging five to seven students, a skilled instructor with the right type of case can engage a large group of students in case discussion. Five key principles undergird the approach at the Harvard Business School (pp. 47–49): importance of situational analysis, making the connection between theoretical knowledge and application/action, active student involvement, shifting the instructor role to teaching students how to learn, and balancing the acquisition of substantive knowledge with the process objectives. An outcome consistent with the school's focus on administration would be for the student to develop an administrative perspective toward business. The development of a multidimensional understanding of a problem, the attention to substance and process, and action orientation are elements consistent with development of a professional social worker and are applicable to education in social work.

In the current educational environment, increasingly students in the professions are taught to perform rather than to think through a strategy before they act. Skill in critical analysis or evaluation of information is often not developed (Rankin, 1999, p. 15). The lack of such thinking and the interest in developing problem-solving skills was one of the observations that led to use of problem-based learning (PBL) in medical education (Savin-Baden, 2000, p. 14). Bruhn (1999, p. 122), in discussing the application of PBL to the allied health professions, emphasizes the importance of producing reflective rather than reactive professionals. He points out further that experience without reflection will not necessarily produce learning (p. 128). Clinical reasoning and decision making requires analytical skills. In social work, use of case studies has also enhanced critical thinking skills (Cossom, 1991).

PROBLEM-BASED LEARNING

Problem situations or cases are jumping-off points for students to search for information. Rangachari (1996, p. 64) refers to them as evocative rather than prescriptive and emphasizes maintaining the balance between substantive and process teaching. Key objectives of the problem-based method are to develop clinical reasoning and problem-solving skills, learn new knowledge and apply it to similar situations, encourage self-directed learning, and enhance motivation to learn through intrinsic interest in the material (Norman and Schmidt, 1992, p. 558).

Detailed steps for the problem-based approach include (1) a clear definition of the problem; (2) tentative formulation; (3) identification of what is known, what knowledge is needed, and the gap in knowledge; (4) identification of learning resources; (5) collection of new information; (6) application of old and new information to the problem; (7) reformulation of the problem and repetition of the previous steps as needed; (8) identification of what was not learned; and (9) testing of the understanding of the knowledge by application to another problem. An additional step used at Harvard, of presenting and teaching material to others, reinforces learning (Burgess, 1992, pp. 4–5).

Barrows (1986) elaborates on the intricacies and nuances in the problem-based learning design. A complete case or a case vignette may be used. There may be either partial or full problem simulation. Learning may be teacher-directed, student-directed, or a combination of both. Depending on how cases are used, they may or may not foster all of the objectives suggested previously. For example, lecture-based cases, or case-based lectures, may not enhance motivation or self-directed learning. However, even a modified case study using small tutorial groups may be designed to meet many of the PBL objectives stated earlier.

Some writers believe this method may better prepare students for clinical contexts (Barrows, 1986). While students must have access to knowledge in order to apply it to problems, the retrieval and application of such knowledge enhances retention and subsequent application. It has been found that students using the PBL method integrate knowledge better than those given direct answers. The importance of immediate discussion and feedback on their insights was emphasized. When students become curious enough about a problem, they may go beyond their own narrow discipline in order to gain knowledge. One of the indicators of success in using the PBL method with medical students was the extent of their use of the library (Rankin, 1999).

COOPERATIVE LEARNING

A group context is the typical approach in using problem-based learning. Groups provide a mix of views, support personal, and social development of students; and can improve skills of listening, self-expression, communication, responding to differences, managing conflict, and development of team cooperation (Burgess, 1992, p. 17). Frequently, students first explore the problem without advance preparation. They discuss their thoughts and observations with other students in their group. Individually and in the group they identify areas for learning in order to help address the problem. There may be individual work between group meetings to gain additional knowledge, which is then shared with the group. Finally, the group reflects on the process and what was learned (Schwartz, Mennin, and Webb, 2001, p. 2).

While the problem-based learning approach in small groups can enhance self-guided learning for individual students, certain factors must be present in order to foster cooperative learning (Duek, 2000; Johnson, Johnson, and Smith, 1991). They include interdependence of group members, assessment of each student's achievement, member diversity, equitable leadership, development of group skills such as communication and conflict resolution, and reflection on the effectiveness of the group. Duek (2000, p. 77) points out that several authors emphasize an underlying model of social interdependence as the essential ingredient for successful group outcomes. Other writers see PBL as a constructivist approach to learning because problems studied are like those found in the real world and because of the emphasis on developing a "learning community" where participants work, converse, and reflect together (Brown and King, 2000, p. 246).

Groups may have high cooperation or low cooperation depending on the level of collaborative interactions. Indeed, groups do not automatically function well; students may need to be taught how to move from individual self-guided learning to group learning (Wilkerson and Gijselaers, 1996, pp. 30, 31). For this reason it is extremely important to orient students to the process at the outset (Wasserman, 1994, pp. 62–63). Such a discussion should include the underlying principles of the method, the difference between PBL and traditional teaching, a clear explication of instructor expectations of students, and awareness of the challenges for students in making the transition.

Not all students will feel that they benefit from this type of learning. They may have difficulty in shifting from a traditional format to one that puts more responsibility on students. Some writers have expressed concern about students receiving misinformation from their student colleagues. Sykes (1990) offers a framework for maximizing success in the use of PBL that is comprised of four structures—conceptual, pedagogical, social, and cognitive. In totality, the four areas address assumptions that help guide the teacher in providing a conceptual framework, an instructional strategy, in development of classroom norms, and in attending to students' knowledge and learning skills. This systematic approach helps to alleviate what Sykes calls the exchange of "anecdotal" knowledge (pp. 299).

A group may be unproductive, lack harmony, or a few students may monopolize the group. Schwartz, Mennin, and Webb (2001, p. 140) found that a group's level of performance is highly dependent on the group's interaction. The teacher or tutor must therefore be alert to the functioning of each group and provide support, refocusing, or additional intervention when needed. This may be done within the group, in individual conferences with students, or by reconstituting a group if necessary (Wasserman, 1994, pp. 68–71).

Evenson and Hmelo (2000) discussed the conclusions of various studies on the use of small tutorial group learning in the problem-based method. One study (p. 30) looked at the effect of prior knowledge on learning in the small group and found that students who had limited knowledge of the subject benefited more from the group discussion than those who read didactic material before the discussion. They retained more by reading the material after the group discussion. Another study that evaluated achievement in relation to verbal participation in the group, found that there was no difference between those participating silently and those who were verbal.

THE TEACHER'S ROLE

Typically, tutors are used as facilitators or resource persons in the small groups (Schwartz, Mennin, and Webb, 2001, p. 2). When tutors are not available for each group, a tutor or class instructor can float from one group to another. The role of the tutor is an important factor in the functioning of the group. Key ingredients for tutor success include both personality/behavior characteristics and group facilitating skills (Holmes and Kaufman, 1999).

The tutor may be directive or nondirective and may or may not have extensive expertise in the subject. Student-guided discussion and selection of issues for focus may be higher in groups with a tutor who is less directive, that is, more passive. Wilkerson and Gijselaers (1996, p. 72) report "the use of tasks with clear procedures and right answers was associated with limited exchange among students, generation of simple explanations, and routine learning." The tutor/teacher who promotes an optimal small group learning environment balances student leadership with tutor assistance, provides learning resources, creates a congenial environment, is enthusiastic and approachable, stimulates critical thinking, addresses group dynamics, and helps to keep the group focused (Wilkerson and Gijselaers, 1996, p. 77; Holmes and Kaufman, 1999, p. 63). Bruhn (1999, p. 124) identifies levels of learning responsibility on a continuum that range from total teacher control over content, with students as passive recipients of knowledge, to student selection of content, with individual and/or group learning contracts and self-initiated use of the teacher as a consultant. The latter model requires that the teacher be willing to give up power and control in the classroom and may take some self-awareness and reflection to accomplish (Wasserman, 1994). Just as not all students are comfortable with problem-based learning, instructors may also have difficulty in making a shift from traditional teaching (Barnes, Christensen, and Hansen, 1994, p. 48). Faculty development may be necessary in order to cultivate the skills needed for this method.

APPLYING THE CASE STUDY METHOD AND PROBLEM-BASED LEARNING TO SOCIAL WORK

There has been little systematic inquiry about the use of the case study method by social workers although writers in other fields have provided us with useful insights into its benefits. Case studies are real examples of practice. Not only are they excellent teaching tools, but the writing and telling of case studies also benefits students, practitioners, and teachers. Teachers who collect case studies keep up-to-date about what is happening in the field. Practitioners who share case studies make a contribution to the education of future professionals.

Students who have learned using the case study method can then reinforce their own learning by turning their own experiences into case studies and teaching other student colleagues.

Because the foundation of social work practice relies on an ecosystems framework, case studies can be fairly complex if they address the many dimensions of a situation. While problem-based learning in both the medical and business settings started out with fairly concise problems, the move to a more holistic approach generated more complex cases. In medicine, students who are learning diagnostic skills can be given a short scenario that they then must analyze to determine what additional information is needed in order to sort out the problem. This may be very similar to the sparse information they may have about patients in an actual clinical environment. Many social work situations are similar to the comprehensive administrative cases used in the Harvard Business School. The cases in this volume, like the business cases and because they are designed to stimulate multilevel thinking, are intentionally complex.

Generally, schools of social work do not have a complete program based on problem-based learning. They also do not provide individual tutors for small group learning. With that in mind, these cases are created so that they can be used flexibly in small or large groups. Students can work on cases completely self-guided without knowing learning objectives or activities in advance, or a more structured format can be used with the learning objectives and activities as a guide. Students and instructors can fashion additional study questions suggested by the cases.

It is important to locate small group problem-based learning in the total learning context in social work. Students will be in the field, they will have assigned readings, didactic material will be presented, and they will have examinations and papers to write. All of these are interrelated. In addition, there will be integration with prerequisite courses and concurrent courses. A combination of self-initiated learning and structured activities, designed to promote integration of content from other parts of the curriculum and to address the learning objectives of a course syllabus, offers a suitable balance. Students will respond differently to the method based on their educational and experience levels. Since social work students both at the undergraduate and graduate levels tend to comprise a mix of experienced and inexperienced, and young and mature students, this diversity will offer benefits and challenges in initiating self-guided and cooperative learning. In my experience and also that of other colleagues, classes can vary in their receptivity to breaking down into small groups on an ongoing basis. At times they want the experience of discussing problems or cases in the larger group, therefore tuning into the group dynamics is important when deciding how to structure the process.

EVIDENCE-BASED PRACTICE

Gambrill (1997, 2000) has advocated for problem-based learning and incorporation of evidence-based practice in social work education. The incorporation of research into the knowledge collection and decision-making process can facilitate critical analysis of the state of knowledge as well as help students evaluate the knowledge they are applying to a problem or case. Evidence-based practice, developed in Great Britain in order to enhance health care decisions, has been incorporated into medical education and medical practice and more recently is being incorporated into social work in Great Britain and the United States (e.g., Corcoran, 2000). Advocates of this approach urge the use of existing research to inform practice and to continue to collect data on what works best. Using evidence can lead to elimination of bias in the evaluation of the effects of interventions and in choice of intervention strategies. The current state of research in social work practice makes it difficult to rely on empirical data, as often there are conflicting findings or little consistent research in a particular area. Corcoran (2000) analyzed research findings on family-based practice in order to provide the most current information on what works best. While there were indications and trends that were helpful in choosing interventions, the lack of comparability in the studies and shortage of replications made it difficult to use as a firm guide. Another example in Britain revealed that the number of controlled research trials done on child protective services to determine what works has been falling (MacDonald, 1998, p. 73). Therefore, current, updated research is not consistently available. Be aware that evidence-based practice is not a substitute for clinical judgment. I believe that qualitative data and analysis of a situation must also be included in decision making.

There are other issues that must be taken into account. Webb (2001) argues from a constructivist perspective and points out that research and the applications of that research cannot be divorced from the agendas of the researchers and the users of the research. For some, evidence means only certain kinds of empirical research that is "objective" and rules out what might be referred to as practice wisdom or qualitative knowledge. Empirical research often does not take into account contextual factors that drive research and enter into social work decision making, such as the political environment in which social work activities and research take place. Witken and Harrison (2001, p. 296) suggest that social workers must think about what benefits and drawbacks there may be to evidence-based practice as it is closely connected to a medical perspective, yet point out that evidence-based practice can move social workers toward more critical thinking about practice and can provide users of service with increased knowledge and tools for empowerment. In this manual, students are encouraged to take research, both quantitative and qualitative, into account in studying cases and at the same time think critically about its limitations. Indeed, the collection of case studies using storytelling and an oral history approach is a form of qualitative data collection (Odell, 2001) that can make a significant contribution to social work practice knowledge.

RECOMMENDED STRATEGIES FOR TEACHING FROM CASE STUDIES IN THIS TEXT

Each case study in this volume includes stated learning objectives, student learning activities, and a list of references that students can turn to if they wish to learn more about the subject. These are all located at the end of the case. Cases are designed for flexibility. Instructors may have students study the case before they read the learning objectives and activities. Instructors may assign all activities for a specific case or selected ones based on the learning objectives they wish to address. Each case has many facets and can be used to teach about specialty areas, specific populations, assessment, interventions, theory, or ethical issues. Cases can also be used to develop analytical and critical thinking skills. While the approach is based on problem-based learning, the activities often go beyond "problem solving" or cognitive solutions to include hands-on experience through role-play or through planning a program.

Learning from case studies is most effective if students read the case at least one week in advance in order to prepare for discussion. Some activities require individual homework in preparation for class discussion. For example, an activity may require researching services for a particular population in the community or may best be addressed after additional reading. Or students can each be responsible for an activity or study question for the next week and take a leadership role on that topic when the group convenes.

Activities and questions are best studied in small groups. Ideal group size is five to seven students. Where subgroups are called for, a minimum of three students should comprise the group. Students may self-select into groups or the instructor can assign students. Students may feel comfortable and tend to stay with a particular group throughout the semester, or they may decide to meet with other students in the class from time to time to get different perspectives. Attention should be paid to experience level and diversity of the group. The instructor monitors participation of each member of the group to ensure that self-guided learning is taking place for every member.

Each case study can take anywhere from one to three hours depending on how many activities are completed. Each group should reflect on what was and was not learned from the case and what other relevant issues they would like to study. Another strategy for reinforcing learning is to have students teach what they learned to other students not in their group. Alternatively, each group could report their deliberations and conclusions to the whole class. Students can also keep a journal reflecting on what they learned from each case study and submit it to the instructor or present it to the group. Students should also reflect on the group process and share ideas for enhancing group functioning.

At times, the instructor may want to involve total class participation by presenting didactic material or posing questions for discussion. This is particularly useful after the small group activities to highlight key learning issues.

REFERENCES

Barnes, L., Christensen, C., and Hansen, A. (1994). *Teaching and the case method.* Boston: Harvard Business School Press.

Barrows, H. (1986). A taxonomy of problem-based learning methods. *Medical Education, 20,* 481–486.

Brown, S., and King, F. (2000). Constructivist pedagogy and how we learn: Educational psychology meets international studies. *International Studies Perspectives, 1,* 245–254.

Bruhn, J. (1999). Problem-based learning: An approach toward reforming allied health education. In J. Rankin, *Handbook on problem-based learning.* New York: Forbes Custom Publishing.

Burgess, H. (1992). *Problem-led learning for social work: The enquiry and action approach.* London: Whiting and Birch.

Corcoran, J. (2000). *Evidence-based social work practice with families: A lifespan approach.* New York: Springer.

Cossom, J. (1991). Teaching from cases: Education for critical thinking. *Journal of Teaching in Social Work, 5,* 139–155.

Devore, W., and Schlesinger, E. (1996). *Ethnic-sensitive social work practice.* Boston: Allyn & Bacon.

Duek, J. (2000). Whose group is it anyway? Equity of student discourse in problem-based learning (PBL). In D. Evensen, and C. Hmelo, *Problem-based learning: A research perspective on learning interactions.* Mahwah, NJ: Erlbaum.

Evensen, D., and Hmelo, C. (2000). *Problem-based learning: A research perspective on learning interactions.* Mahwah, NJ: Erlbaum.

Gambrill, E. (1997). *Social work practice: A critical thinker's guide.* New York: Oxford University Press.

Gambrill, E. (2000). *The role of critical thinking in evidence-based social work.* In P. Allen-Meares, and C. Garvin, *The handbook of social work direct practice.* Thousand Oaks, CA: Sage.

Holmes, B., and Kaufman, D. (1999). Tutoring in problem-based learning: A teacher development process. In J. Rankin, *Handbook on problem-based learning.* New York: Forbes Custom Publishing.

Johnson, D., Johnson, R., and Smith, K. (1991). Cooperative learning: Increasing college faculty instructional productivity. ASHE-ERIC Higher Education Report NO. 4. Washington, DC: George Washington University, School of Education and Human Development.

Kemp, S. (1995). Practice with communities. In C. Meyer, and M. Mattaini (Eds.), *The foundations of social work practice.* Washington, DC: NASW Press.

Kirst-Ashman, K., and Hull, G. (1999). The macro skills workbook: A generalist approach. Chicago: Nelson-Hall.

Landon, P., and Feit, M. (1999). *Generalist social work practice.* Daybook, IA: Eddie Bowers.

LeCroy, W. (1999). *Case studies in social work practice.* Pacific Grove, CA: Brooks/Cole.

MacDonald, G. (1998). Promoting evidence-based practice in child protection. *Clinical Child Psychology and Psychiatry, 3,* 71–85.

McNair, M. (1954). *The case method at the Harvard business school.* New York: McGraw-Hill.

Norman, G., Schmidt, H. (1992). The psychological basis of problem-based learning: A review of the evidence. *Academic Medicine, 67,* 557–565.

Odell, J. (2001). Case study methods in international political economy. *International Studies Perspectives, 2,* 161–176.

Rangachari, P. (1996). Twenty-up: Problem-based learning with a large group. In L. Wilkerson, and W. Gijselaers, *Bringing problem-based learning to higher education: Theory and practice.* San Francisco: Jossey-Bass.

Rankin, J. (1999). *Handbook on problem-based learning.* New York: Forbes Custom Publishing.

Rivas, R., and Hull, G. (1996). *Case studies in generalist practice.* Pacific Grove, CA: Brooks/Cole.

Savin-Baden, M. (2000). *Problem-based learning in higher education: Untold stories.* Buckingham, UK: The Society for Research into Higher Education and Open University Press.

Schwartz, P., Mennin, S., and Webb, G. (2001). *Problem-based learning: Case studies, experience, and practice.* London: Kogan Page.

Sykes, G. (1990). Learning to teach with cases. *Journal of Policy Analysis and Management, 9,* 297–302.

Tropman, J., and Richards-Schuster, K. (2000). *The concept of levels and systems in social work.* In C. Garvin, and P. Allen-Meares, *The handbook of social work direct practice* (pp. 65–84). Thousand Oaks, CA: Sage.

Wasserman, S. (1994). *Introduction to case method teaching.* New York: Teachers College Press.

Webb, S. A. (2001). Some considerations on the validity of evidence-based practice in social work. *British Journal of Social Work, 31,* 57–79.

Wilkerson, L., and Gijselaers, W. (1996). *Bringing problem-based learning to higher education: Theory and practice.* San Francisco: Jossey-Bass.

Witken, S., and Harrison, D. (2001). Whose evidence and for what purpose? *Social Work, 46,* 293–296.

CHAPTER TWO

MULTILEVEL WORK WITH INDIVIDUALS AND FAMILIES

INTRODUCTION

This chapter comprises five cases—three focusing on adults, one on a couple, and one case that addresses the interaction between organizational policy and services and a family with a child experiencing emotional problems. Interventions include individual, family, group, organizational change, and community education. Theoretical frameworks include the strengths perspective; solution-focused and narrative approaches; cognitive-behavioral, psychoanalytic, intersubjective, task-oriented, and family systems; and empowerment and feminist theories. Cases 2-1 and 2-3 focus on development of self-awareness with activities designed to raise consciousness about countertransference issues. Clinical and organizational ethics are raised in Cases 2-3 and 2-5, respectively. This chapter addresses special topics such as the effects of family abuse and sexual trauma (Case 2-3), homelessness in adults with mental illness (Case 2-4), and work with children and families who are affected by attention-deficit disorder (Case 2-5). Case 2-2 provides an opportunity to gain an understanding of Latino culture and to study culturally sensitive interventions. Case 2-3 allows the student to explore in depth how best to deal with referring and transferring clients. Case 2-4 addresses the interface between homelessness and mental illness.

2-1 STRENGTHS-BASED AND SOLUTION-FOCUSED NARRATIVE INTERVENTION

DAVID NYLUND

Introduction

In this case study, students are introduced to a short-term narrative approach to treatment that includes solution-focused techniques. Narratives are not frequently presented to students, therefore, samples of the narratives are included in order to make the work more vivid. Students can focus on three perspectives to treatment—strengths-based, solution-focused, and narrative. The therapist is directive, has an idiosyncratic style—which for some is nontraditional—and provides an opportunity for students to learn new techniques as well as to think about and compare their own use of self with clients. The abuse issues in the case call on students to examine their own reactions and to determine ways in which their reactions can impact their work. The case demonstrates the use of a short-term approach to address problems that have existed for many years and can be used to consider other treatment options for comparison that may be of longer duration. While the case describes one level of treatment, students are asked to consider the pros and cons of family and group approaches for this client/client system. The case includes detailed examples of narratives constructed by the therapist that summarize the client's progress.

Case Study

The setting is an outpatient mental health service. Stacey is a thirty-seven-year-old Caucasian woman brought up in a strict Mormon family. She has one sister, age thirty-two, and a brother, age twenty-nine. During the initial session, Stacey and Mike, her social worker, discussed her fear of people at work and at the grocery store. She talked about beatings she had received throughout her childhood. Her parents felt that children should be seen and not heard. Furthermore, Stacey's father told her that if she told her school counselor about the abuse, he would kill her. Aspects of Stacey's life had been overtaken by shame, guilt, depression, and self-doubt.

After the first session, Mike wrote Stacey the following letter:

Dear Stacey,

You quite painfully and vividly shared some of the stories and events of your life and childhood. I thought it took courage in doing so and you agreed by saying, "Yes, because I know I need help." Your parents have been influenced by some old ideas that children . . . should be seen and not heard, and that children's voices are not to be respected; the parent's voice rules with an iron fist and that you are to serve your parents. Understandably, this coached you into a life of guilt and servitude. The secrecy of your family, as enforced by threat of more abuse by your father, was enforced in a very dictatorial manner. This secrecy must have made it hard to believe in a future for yourself, and yet, as I said in the meeting, I wonder if there were some small, subtle, or covert ways that you resisted the abuse and believed that what your parents were doing to you was unjust. Lately, the sense of injustice is beginning to express itself in some healthy, creative, and rebellious ways. Some of these steps include not paying the rent, going to counseling, wearing the clothes that you prefer, not going home directly, and going shopping and going out with friends from work.

This reminds me, Stacey: What do your friends appreciate about you to which your parents are, and have been, blind? If you were to side further with your friends' view of you, what effect might this have on further escape from guilt? Again, I was very honored to meet you. To my way of thinking, you are a heroine who does not know her own heroism. I very much look forward to helping you rewrite your history and carve out a future for yourself, a liberating future.

Sincerely,

Mike M.

As the next two appointments passed, Mike continued to support Stacey in overcoming the guilt and getting an upper hand on fear. Stacey was beginning to be more assertive as well. She began to stand up for herself more at work and was becoming close friends with Corey, a co-worker. Corey was familiar both with problems in the workplace and with having healed her own "abused innerchild." Corey became, over several weeks, an avid advocate, supporter, and friend for Stacey. Abused as a child herself, and having managed depression in young adulthood, Corey was a powerful ally in assisting Stacey in getting the upper hand on self-doubt and guilt. Stacey began making statements that reflected newfound strength in her gender identity as a woman and in her ability to act assertively.

After their third session, Mike wrote the following news release:

STACEY'S NEWS RELEASE

Stacey slaps GUILT around! Is envisioning Her own freedom! Embraces self-care!

Marvin Gardens, July 21, 1994: Stacey, aged 37, from Regal Heights, was tyrannized by GUILT. GUILT had her imprisoned and voiceless. Now she is beginning to weather the storm of GUILT by:

- making friends such as Corey, who coach her into anti-guilt.
- looking for her own apartment.
- talking to her sister and breaking through the oppressive secrecy that got in the way of their sisterhood.
- reading biographies of heroic and courageous women such as Betsy Ross and Harriet Pitman.
- meeting covertly with Mike, anti-guilt consultant and covert resister.

Stacey was asked what was enabling her to witness her own freedom, and she replied with a smile, "I'm ignoring the GUILT and pushing it away. I have to do what is right for me. . . . I can't live for others anymore!" At the fifth session, Stacey reported several significant steps she has taken toward claiming her freedom and power. She has been silent at home. This has been an effective, peaceful protest against family enmeshment, secrecy, and a hollow homeostasis. Standing for her needs, against her mother's disapproval, Stacey has signed up for classes at the junior college. Stacey also told her mom, "I can't live like this anymore." As she gained power, Stacey sobbed and sobbed about the abuse she had sustained. Experiencing a new sense of self brought the contrast between the injustices Stacey had tolerated in her home life and the newly identified personal potential. By the end of the fifth session, Stacey was able to identify strengths she has as a resilient woman who has survived tremendous physical and emotional abuse. Also, Stacey was able to identify how some of this personal strength arose from learning her mother's survival skills.

Toward the end of the sixth session, Stacey was able to make consistent eye contact and make many positive self-statements. She acknowledged how deep her pain had been and how she had begun to get the upper hand on The Guilt and was learning how to "stand up for what I know is right." While Stacey sometimes doubted herself, she clearly had made significant progress.

The seventh session was conducted as a team session. Stacey and Mike sat in front of a one-way mirror and Corey, Stacey's friend from work, joined them. Several colleagues observed the interview from behind the mirror. They also videotaped the session. Because this video was to be used for future training purposes, Mike was more directive than he might otherwise have been—as he wished to make several points. Corey was very generous in her appreciation, support, and caring for Stacey during this session. Although Stacey had made significant growth in getting the upper hand on The Guilt, as a Freedom Fighter, and in standing up for herself in a variety of situations, she still came off as shy during the videotaping.

Following the seventh and last session, Mike wrote this final letter to Stacey:

Dear Stacey,

I really appreciated your courage in attending today's team meeting with your friend Corey. I inquired about your courage and right away Corey told me about an inspiring step that you took at the office, submitting a grievance requesting necessary training that had not been provided by your current employer. She was quite proud of you, and this moved you to tears as you had just talked about how much she cares for you and how important it is to have somebody love you. I inquired as to whether this means that you are feeling more entitled to being cared for. As the session continued, more inspiring anti-guilt steps occurred. One of your most famous quotable quotes from this session was, "I am not a robot anymore." Now that you are not a robot, how do you see yourself? What do you think you are stepping into? Lastly, from a vantage point in the future, what new directions were made possible by what you have recently discovered about yourself? How do these realizations and conclusions make it possible for you to intervene in your future and in what ways? In closing, Stacey, again the team and I were moved by witnessing your continued journey into freedom and personhood. As I said, it is as if a heroine does not appreciate her own heroism. Corey, thanks for attending the session. We were touched by your friendship.

Mike has heard from Stacey once or twice over the years, just checking in for a "tune-up," and as her life provides exciting opportunities for growth and change, she is continuing to expand her sense of possibilities.

LEARNING OBJECTIVES

1. Understand and apply the strengths perspective to short-term solution-focused work with an individual using a narrative approach.

2. Compare and contrast the ways in which short- and long-term approaches are used and set treatment goals for each based on case information.

3. Critically evaluate a sequence of interventions, identifying strengths and areas you would do differently.

4. Demonstrate skill in determining appropriateness of combining individual, family, and/or group interventions.

5. Explain your countertransference reactions and describe ways of dealing with them.

ACTIVITIES

1. Identify the characteristics of the strengths-based, solution-focused, and narrative interventions in the case. What are your thoughts about the effectiveness of these interventions for Stacey? Would you do anything differently? Using role-play with another group member, demonstrate how you would intervene with Stacey using one of these perspectives.

2. Describe Mike's therapeutic style. In what ways is it similar to or different from your own style?

3. This case is an example of short-term treatment. What was accomplished through the sessions with Stacey? Would you have recommended additional sessions? If so, what goals would you set if you could conduct twelve sessions? twenty sessions? Defend your position based on evidence in the case.

4. Would you consider family and/or group interventions for Stacey? Discuss the pros and cons of each. How and when would you include them, and with what goals in mind?

5. Keeping in mind your own background, what feelings and thoughts do you have related to Stacey's abuse? How would this affect your work with Stacey? If you decided to include Stacey's mother and father in your intervention plan, in what ways might your own experiences and attitudes help or hinder your work with them?

SUGGESTED READINGS

Abels, P., and Abels, S. (Eds.). (2001). *Understanding narrative therapy: A guidebook for the social worker.* New York: Springer.

Cowger, C. (1994). Assessing client strengths: Clinical assessment for client empowerment. *Social Work, 39,* 288–296.

Freedman, J., and Combs, G. (1996). *Narrative therapy: The social construction of preferred realities.* New York: Norton.

Saleeby, D. (1992). *The strengths perspective in social work practice.* New York: Longman.

2-2   RAUL AND NORA: A LATINO COUPLE IN TRANSITION

Introduction

This case provides an opportunity for students to explore the impact of current and past psychosocial stressors on a marriage. The couple is struggling with recent traumatic events that have disrupted their marriage and brought ongoing dissatisfaction to the surface. Students explore key issues in couples work—communication, intimacy, sexuality, and confidentiality. The husband and wife have different levels of commitment to the counseling process. The student is challenged to manage the process, including the question of seeing the couple together or separately. In order to fully understand role expectations in this marriage, the student needs to gain an understanding of Mexican culture and how gender roles are interpreted. Additionally, the student must examine how to interact with the clients in a culturally sensitive way. Students must figure out how to manage the interview process and to assist the couple in improving their communication. Students can sharpen their skills in dealing with sensitive issues such as abuse and sexual relations. Multilevel interventions addressed in the case include individual, couple, and community interventions. Applicable theories are ecosystems, family systems, cognitive-behavioral, feminist, and empowerment.

Case Study

Raul and Nora Guadalupe sought help at a mental health center due to multiple life stressors that have impacted their marriage. Subsequent to a coercive traumatic sexual relationship with a respected physician in their community, Nora was hospitalized for a psychotic break. Nora reported that she had been stalked, brainwashed, and raped by this man. She was unable to work for two years. Following several months of intensive outpatient care, Nora realized that her marriage was lacking. During the intake session, it became clear that there were long-standing marital issues regarding communication, roles, intimacy, and sexuality.

Both Nora and Raul grew up in poverty. Nora has an extensive history of child abuse, and Raul experienced some physical abuse as a child. Additional stressors include Raul's long work hours and a recent burglary in which the couple's house suffered significant damage and many belongings were stolen.

The couple, both in their forties, are of Mexican background, although Raul is American born. Santiago, their twenty-year-old son, is away at a well-regarded small college. Their daughter, Yolanda, who is nineteen, lives at home and is planning to be married. Nora, although trained as a physical therapist, runs a gift shop. Raul, in response to financial needs, has been working about two hours from their semi-rural home in a small city. He stays overnight at his job location four nights per week. Raul also works part-time on the weekend at another job once a month.

With the limited time they spend together on the weekends, Raul and Nora often fight while working to improve the aesthetic presentation of Nora's store or repairing their damaged home. Throughout the past two years, when Nora was unable to work, Raul has paid rent for the store space. Raul works the night shift at his full-time job so that transition to normal sleep-wake hours on the weekends is nearly impossible, and he is very sleep-deprived.

Initially, the couple came to the sessions together. After four sessions, Nora stated that she preferred not to attend on a regular basis. Most sessions now, Raul comes alone, though at times Nora also attends. Raul has been working on marital issues, focusing on communication and his sexual relationship with Nora. As a result of overwork, lack of sleep, and the vicarious trauma Raul has experienced in relation to Nora's abuse by the other man, Raul is emotionally overwhelmed, often challenged, and unable to express his feelings clearly. Another stressor is that both parents dislike their daughter's choice of partner but disagree on how to handle it. Raul has been forthright in stating his dislike, however, Nora has refrained in the interest of maintaining her relationship with their daughter.

Nora feels abandoned by her husband emotionally and sexually. She wishes he were more available and is upset that he is not. Nora, in couples sessions, has expressed anger toward Raul for his absence, emotional distance, and lack of desire for intimate contact including sensual and sexual contact. One year prior to therapy, Nora told her husband that intercourse with him was painful. For the next year, Raul did not initiate sex and avoided intercourse. After beginning counseling, Nora told Raul that she had lied and was actually not sexually interested that evening. Raul feels shame and guilt regarding his situation and further beaten down by the added stress of Nora's judgments and criticisms.

In counseling Raul has been encouraged to look at his feelings and his personal needs. Repeatedly, issues regarding caring, contact, intimacy, and sexual contact with Nora have been explored. With his wife, at this time, Raul is experiencing lack of drive and impotence. Raul has begun to take steps toward self-care, including quitting his weekend job and diminishing his list of tasks over the weekends. The couple is now meeting once a week halfway between Raul's work and their home. Raul is beginning to explore intimacy with Nora though she continues to be impatient and critical.

LEARNING OBJECTIVES

1. Increase knowledge and skill in working with couples.
   a. Enhance client communication skills.
   b. Deal sensitively with intimacy and sexuality.
   c. Manage confidentiality.
2. Understand gender expectations in a marriage in the context of culture.
3. Apply feminist and empowerment theories.
4. Understand the impact of socioeconomic factors on marital dynamics.

ACTIVITIES

1. Using role-play with other students in your group, conduct an interview with Raul and Nora in order to determine specifically the nature of their sexual problem/ interaction and their feelings about it. Intervene to help them become conscious of communication patterns and to improve them during the interview.

2. Discuss any challenges for you in addressing intimate matters.

3. Do you see any human diversity (age, gender, ethnic, socioeconomic, etc.) issues present in this case that impact the couple's situation and would affect your assessment?

4. Discuss specific goals and objectives for this case and how you would determine whether they have been met. Present these to student colleagues in your group.

5. What treatment options would you consider to help them improve their sexual relationship?

6. What theoretical perspectives and intervention modalities do you see as most effective in working with this couple given the nature of their stress, distress, and cultural considerations? How would you incorporate feminist and empowerment theories?

7. How you would manage the issue of whether the couple is seen together or individually. What would you tell the couple about how you would handle confidentiality?

8. What group or community interventions might you consider to assist couples in similar situations, and what steps would you take to implement them?

SUGGESTED READINGS

Falicov, C. (1998). *Latino families in therapy: A guide to multicultural practice.* New York: Guilford.

Irving, I., Benjamin, M., and San-Pedro, J. (1999). Family mediation and cultural diversity: Mediating with Latino families. *Mediation Quarterly, 16,* 325–338.

2-3   CLINICAL PRACTICE IN A RURAL COMMUNITY WITH AN ADULT SURVIVOR OF SEXUAL TRAUMA

JANICE R. GAGERMAN

Introduction

This case scenario focuses on therapeutic dilemmas experienced by a social worker in private practice in a rural community. Key issues are countertransference and professional self-awareness as they affect the therapeutic process and clinical decisions. In this case, the social worker must terminate with the client due to changes in the worker's job responsibilities and describes her emotional struggles about having to do this. Students can discuss the impact of their own feelings on their practice and what they must do to handle these professionally. The question of transfer of clients presents an opportunity for exploring how to expedite this in a way that is best for the client. Ethical issues that are raised include boundary issues in a rural community, obligations to provide pro bono services, and the pros and cons of providing individual and group services by the same therapist. Applicable theoretical frameworks are psychoanalytic theory, intersubjectivity, task-oriented interventions, and trauma theory. Students become sensitive to practice issues with clients who have been sexually abused and can explore the psychodynamic aspects of sexual abuse. They become familiar with the use of the DSM-IV TR as a diagnostic tool.

Case Study

Helene, a thirty-seven-year-old Caucasian woman, was a social worker who worked for Children's Protective Services (CPS). Eight years ago, Helene attended a workshop on childhood trauma conducted by Karen Marcus, a clinical social worker who was highly regarded within her small rural community of Opal. The workshop had considerable impact on Helene. She enrolled in order to enhance her knowledge and skill as a child protective worker but also found that it stirred up personal issues related to her own childhood. Following Karen's presentation, Helene approached Karen and, after a gracious compliment regarding the workshop, Helene stated that she would like to begin therapy with Karen.

Shortly thereafter, Karen and Helene met for the first session. Helene discussed the personal difficulties she was having with her husband. She also mentioned the emotional abuse and neglect she had experienced during childhood. Karen informed Helene that she was forming a group for women who have histories of child abuse. The group would focus on current issues in their relationships with partners, children, friends, and employers. Although it is unusual for a new client to be enthusiastic about sharing difficult issues in a group, Karen's new group was highly appealing to Helene. They continued individual work until the group started a month later.

The group met weekly for six months for a total of twenty-four sessions. They first contracted for eight weeks and then negotiated for two more eight-week time periods. The group started with five women and then continued with four in the last two eight-week periods. In the first group session, where Karen employed a sentence completion exercise to structure the group process work, Helene described her husband as a wonderful, caring man. The group went well for Helene, who did significant work. She was able to discuss issues that she had not previously addressed. She revealed that she had been abused and molested by her mother's boyfriend. In discussing her relationship with her husband, Helene described splitting from herself when hugging and fully removing herself, or dissociating, while having sex with him.

With the support of the group members, and with the other women sharing their histories of childhood abuse, Helene eventually disclosed much of her own abuse history in the group. During group treatment, the women reported dreams that were emerging. In session thirteen, Helene reported that one night last week she woke up from a dream and grabbed her husband's throat, choking his windpipe, screaming the name "Ben." She then had an urge to eat/swallow a lot of bananas, which she did, while still half asleep, stuffing them down her throat. After a pause, she told the group that when she puts cream on her dry face, the sensation becomes very sexual. At that moment, Helene "got a flash" that "Ben" probably was spreading the semen on her face, which she tied to an experience several weeks ago about "wanting to vomit up a lot of shit" after putting cream on her face. After a few moments, Helene told the group she believes she probably was forced into oral sex, and that she wanted to spit up the semen. During the story, Helene began crying, hiding her face. She became full of rage, and said she wished she knew who "Ben" was. If she did, she was sure she would find him and kill him.

At the end of the fifth month, Karen was offered a high-level position at a county mental health agency and announced to the group that she would need to significantly reduce her private practice in one month's time. This coincided with the termination of the group. Clinically, this activated earlier loss and abandonment issues Helene experienced from childhood, expressed through depression and suicide ideation. Helene became suicidal. Karen saw Helene individually in order to respond to the crisis and initiated a task-centered treatment plan to address the suicidal ideations. Karen established a suicide prevention agreement. Helene agreed to have her husband watch over her while she attended her son's high school graduation. The next night Helene was drinking heavily and she agreed, over the phone, to enter inpatient treatment the following morning.

Since it was necessary for Helene to be absent from her work, Karen, with Helene's permission, contacted Helene's supervisor and was able to obtain a three-month leave without pay for Helene. The supervisor was aware of Karen's reputation as a therapist and trusted her professional judgment without asking for details. Karen had worked with this CPS supervisor when employed some years prior at a foster family agency. Thus, a professional relationship had been previously established between the two of them. Information about Helene's inpatient treatment was also kept confidential from the other CPS workers at her place of employment.

At the hospital, Helene was given the following diagnoses:

Axis I—309.89 PTSD (Post Traumatic Stress Disorder),
    Rule out 300.14 (Dissociative Identity Disorder),
    311.00 Depressive reaction associated with suicidal ideation and intent, recent suicide attempt, profound feeling of hopelessness and helplessness regarding early childhood trauma,
    305.00 Alcohol abuse

Axis II—V799.91 (diagnosis deferred)

Axis III—History of Heart Murmur

Axis IV—Occupational problems, problems with family

Axis V—Discharge, 65

Medication prescription: Paxil 40 mg.

Aftercare transition group, 4 weeks.

After Helene's release from inpatient care and a few more individual sessions, Karen conducted a transfer session to another Licensed Clinical Social Worker (LCSW) because, due to her new job, she was unable to provide the level of care Helene needed. Karen, Helene, and the new LCSW spent two hours in session together, providing as best a transfer experience as possible given the difficult situation and presenting problems. Karen felt awful transferring Helene. She felt that, although she was making a reasonable and well-thought-out professional decision, she was abandoning Helene. Helene, subsequently, did not stay with the new practitioner, whose affective style was different from Karen's. She had psychologically attached to Karen, and a new practitioner was too different and too difficult for Helene to attach to at this point in time.

In 1997, at the request of another group member, Karen reconvened the women's group in which Helene had participated four years prior. Helene was excited to work with the group again. She had become divorced and was working in a field using computer technology. She reported hanging out in bars quite a bit and engaging in "one-night stands" with various men. At the conclusion of the group, Karen again worked individually with Helene. Because of Helene's extreme financial struggle, Karen offered pro bono services. Through individual therapy with Karen, Helene was able to refocus her life and make decisions that provided more stability and satisfaction for herself, her work, and her relationships. Karen's goals, interventions, and practice theories were informed by task-centered and intersubjective/self psychology approaches to treatment. She also supported Helene in her decision to significantly decrease alcohol use and abuse.

Helene's son John moved back to his mother's house. John was very angry and upset with how his mother's instability had been impacting his life. Helene made progress in her individual therapy. She met a new boyfriend through her work, Louis, who was kind, caring, and gentle. Even though she knew that this would be a temporary relationship with Louis for a variety of reasons, it was a significant step for her to be able to accept this nurturing and warm friendship.

Over time Helene saved enough money to accomplish her dream of traveling to France. She went for six months and upon returning formalized the conclusion of her previous relationship. She resumed individual therapy with Karen for several weeks in order to "check in," which assisted Helene in connecting with, sustaining, and managing her affective needs. Helene has been able to substantially change her life and to clearly identify healthy goals, needs, and desires; and will be returning to France to live.

Thus, Karen recognized her additional stresses, workload, and anxieties when taking on a new job, in addition to meeting her family obligations. This self-awareness contributed to her decision to transfer Helene to another LCSW who could provide the necessary level of care. Four years later, Karen had moved to another stage in her life where she was comfortable in her job, which was no longer new, and due to changes in her family situation had more time to devote to private practice and to be available as a clinician to provide treatment for Helene at the level she needed. Karen understood that countertransference issues can change over time, and in her case were impacted by her life stage, new job opportunity, and familial obligations.

LEARNING OBJECTIVES

1. Increase self-awareness and understanding of countertransference issues and how to address them.

2. Coordinate multiple interventions with a client.

3. Develop advanced skills in conducting client transfers and referrals.

4. Develop clinical decision-making skills regarding choice of interventions with adult survivors of sexual abuse, child abuse, and trauma.

5. Increase knowledge of ethical and boundary considerations in small communities.

ACTIVITIES

1. Helene reports a history of sexual trauma throughout her childhood.

   a. Explain how the Axis I DSM-IV TR diagnosis presented in the case would facilitate and/or hinder your treatment plan for the client.
   b. In working with adults who have experienced sexual trauma, what does the research show regarding the most effective approaches? How might

you use the task-centered and intersubjective approaches to assist this client?

2. Karen worked individually and in a group with Helene. What are the arguments for and against providing services to clients individually and in a group? How would you coordinate these two treatment modalities if you were the worker in both situations? How would you coordinate if another worker were providing one of the interventions?

3. Discuss Karen's decision to transfer Helene based on her new professional obligations that significantly decreased her time for private practice. During your time as a student, you may have experienced significant life changes or events. How have these events impacted your fieldwork, and which countertransferences do you need to be especially aware of at this time?

4. Referral and transfer of cases require skills to ensure a smooth transition. What would you address in a transfer session with Helene, taking into account her specific situation and general good social work practice?

5. Karen conducted a private practice in a small rural town. In what ways did she maintain boundaries while at the same time acting in the interests of her client? How would you handle chance meetings with a client in this small town? What norms, rules, and ethics guide you in making decisions about nonclinical contacts and personal relationships with clients?

6. Karen decided to provide pro bono services to Helene. Discuss the social worker's ethical responsibility as stated in the NASW Code of Ethics. Under what circumstances would you provide such services, when would you not provide them?

SUGGESTED READINGS

American Psychiatric Association. (2000). *Diagnostic and statistical manual of mental disorders* (4th ed., Text Rev.). Washington, DC: Author.

Chenot, D. (1998). Self psychology, intersubjectivity, and social work. *Clinical Social Work Journal, 26,* 297–311.

Corey, G., Corey, M., and Callanan, P. (2003). Managing boundaries and multiple relationships. In *Issues and ethics in the helping professions* (6th ed., pp. 244–289). Pacific Grove, CA: Brooks/Cole.

Epstein, L. (1988). *Helping people: The task-centered approach.* Columbus, OH: Merrill.

Gagerman, J. (1997). Integrating dream analysis with intersubjectivity in group psychotherapy. *Clinical Social Work Journal, 25,* 163–178.

Goldstein, E. (1994). Self-disclosure in treatment: What therapists do and don't talk about. *Clinical Social Work Journal, 22,* 417–433.

Goldstein, E. (1997). To tell or not to tell: The disclosure of events in the therapist's life to the patient. *Clinical Social Work Journal, 25,* 41–58.

Goldstein, E., and Noonan, M. (1999). *Short-term treatment and social work practice: An integrative perspective.* New York: Free Press.

Herman, J. (1992). *Trauma and recovery.* New York: Basic Books.

National Association of Social Workers. (1997). *Code of ethics.* Washington, DC: Author.

Stern, D. (1985). *The interpersonal world of the infant.* New York: Basic Books.

Strean, H. (1996). Psychoanalytic treatment and social work practice. In F. Turner (Ed.), *Social work treatment: Interlocking theoretical approaches.* New York: Simon and Shuster.

2-4 ASSESSMENT CHALLENGES WITH AN ADULT HOMELESS MALE

Introduction

This case study demonstrates the significant challenges that can arise in the process of developing an accurate assessment for an older adult who has had chronic emotional difficulties and is away from home and apart from his family. The client appears to have income yet presents at a homeless shelter. The worker is faced with a number of contradictory pieces of information and must determine how to put together pieces of a puzzle into a coherent explanation of the client's situation. The case provides students with an opportunity to delve into the complexities of diagnosis and the process of diagnostic decision making. The fact that the client appears to have several conditions makes this even more challenging. The primary intervention method illustrated is cognitive-behavioral/reality-centered work with adult individuals. Mobilization of resources and case management also are relevant. The case suggests resource and program needs for a population of dependent adults, therefore, students can move to another level of intervention, which is population-focused, and also practice their program development skills. The situation described counters the typical impression that homeless people are poor and demonstrates that homelessness can be due to a variety of causes; therefore, students can gain a greater understanding of this social problem. Applicable theoretical frameworks are cognitive-behavioral theory, ecosystems, and family systems.

Case Study

Ben is a white male in his early fifties, born and raised in the Northwest. The client was referred to a local mental health clinic at a homeless complex. He had told an outreach worker from the homeless shelter that he wanted to be hospitalized in a mental hospital and requested assistance in being admitted. The worker explained that they could admit him involuntarily if he was a danger to himself or others, but that first he needed to be evaluated at the mental health center.

  After an initial screening, Ben was referred to the social worker for a biopsychosocial assessment. He reported that he was sleeping in his van (which appeared to be rather new) in the shelter parking lot. He seemed to be much better dressed than the usual homeless population at the shelter. He was wearing slacks, a button-down shirt, and a leather jacket. He was also well groomed, clean-shaven, and recently had a haircut. He told the worker that he was using the shower facilities at the shelter and was eating lunches in the dining room.

  A mental status exam revealed that the client's orientation was good; he seemed alert and aware of his location, knew who the current president was, and also knew the day and month. Ben spoke in a slow, monosyllabic drawl, often stopping in mid-sentence or just trailing off. He had a blank stare, and it sometimes seemed like he wasn't listening. His speech and thought content were nondelusional, his mood was flat, and his affect was constricted. He told the social worker several times that he was extremely depressed and anxious and often changed position in his chair. The social worker recommended a referral to the psychiatrist. Although Ben was not very open about discussing his past, he did relate that he had seen a psychiatrist a few years ago and had been diagnosed but could not remember what his diagnosis was. Since he already had a diagnosis, the worker gave him a referral to another agency for a psychiatric evaluation and possible medication. The mental health clinic at the homeless facility could continue to work with him after he was evaluated.

The client was referred back to the mental health clinic after a futile attempt by the triage nurse to gain enough information to develop a diagnosis. The social worker was then able to schedule an appointment with the mental health clinic psychiatrist. The social worker accompanied Ben to the session with Dr. Kim. The client seemed much more relaxed and talkative. He stated that he had been living with his mother for some time, but she had died and he had nowhere else to go. He said he wanted to get help for his mental problems and eventually make a new start, maybe even get a job. He said all this without showing much emotion, still looking depressed and talking in a monosyllabic way.

The social worker asked him to provide the name and address of his last doctor. At first he didn't answer, but after the psychiatrist asked him a second time, he gave the name of the doctor and the clinic he last visited. The psychiatrist then asked that he sign a release of information so that they could send for his records. He looked startled for a moment and then said he wasn't sure he wanted to do that. Dr. Kim said that was fine but didn't think they could help him with what little information they had gotten from him so far. The client signed two releases of information to be sent to his last doctor and clinic. Dr. Kim prescribed Prozac (antidepressant) and Zyprexa (antipsychotic) and recommended social work follow-up in one week. Dr. Kim's diagnostic impression was Axis I—Schizophrenia undifferentiated type, Axis II—Dependent personality.

The client's former psychiatrist telephoned and informed the social worker that the client's mother was not dead but had been in an accident and had brain damage, which made her unable to handle her affairs. The client's sister was trying to get conservatorship of the mother's estate and had also tried (unsuccessfully) to gain conservatorship of Ben. Ben became distressed by this effort, and it was partly over this that he disappeared. His psychiatrist suggested that the social worker contact the mother's accountant for further information about the financial situation and provided the phone number.

The accountant reported that Ben's stepfather had left a great deal of money to his wife and that Ben himself had $300,000 in assets. The family tried to initiate the conservatorship proceedings when the client allegedly went on a spending spree two years ago and spent several thousand dollars. The accountant was evasive and terminated the conversation when the social worker requested verification in writing of those assets.

Information provided in writing from the last mental health agency that provided services to the client revealed the following history. Over the years, and as far back as elementary school, the client had been diagnosed as brain-injured, autistic, schizophrenic, developmentally delayed, and as a malingerer. Ben graduated high school and has been involved with various mental health clinics ever since. He has lived with his mother his entire life, being completely dependent on her. He has been socially isolated, has no friends, and has never been employed.

Ben sees the social worker once a week. He provides counseling, has provided shelter for him, has encouraged him to apply for Supplemental Security Income, and is trying to help him gain access to his assets. Ben resists making decisions for himself, and a recurrent theme is how he wants to be taken care of. He has even thought about shoplifting in the hope that he will be caught and sent to jail to be housed and fed. He refuses to have anything to do with his family or former home. He does not seem to want to help himself, yet he is likeable and able to get others to do things for him. He responds to a cognitive-behavioral and reality-based approach to his thoughts and behaviors. If he is forced to live on the streets he will not survive.

LEARNING OBJECTIVES

1. Conduct a comprehensive biopsychosocial assessment.

2. Make a differential diagnosis.

3. Based on the assessment and diagnosis, develop an intervention plan.

4. Move from client to program focus.

ACTIVITIES

1. How do biological, psychological, and socioeconomic factors explain this situation? What other information would be helpful to you, and how would you go about gathering it? Given what you know, what would be a coherent assessment of this situation?

2. What evidence in the case supports or negates the diagnostic categories chosen by Dr. Kim? Discuss other diagnostic categories that you might consider, and explain to your colleagues why you would rule them in or out.

3. Based on research, what interventions would work best with the diagnostic category you believe best fits Ben?

4. Ben's mother has been his primary source of support throughout his adulthood. What services are available in your community for an adult whose caretaker is no longer able to provide care. If you were to design a program for such adults, what would you include?

SUGGESTED READINGS

American Psychiatric Association. (2000). *Diagnostic and statistical manual of mental disorders* (4th ed., Text Rev.).Washington, DC: Author.

Austrian, S. (2000). *Mental disorders, medication, and clinical social work* (2nd ed., Chapter 6—Schizophrenia, pp. 93–115; Chapter 9—Personality disorders, pp. 175–213). New York: Columbia University Press.

Gitterman, A. (2001*). Social work practice with vulnerable and resilient populations* (Chapter 10—Schizophrenia, pp. 275–304). New York: Columbia University Press.

Walsh, J. (2000). *Clinical case management with persons having mental illness.* Belmont, CA: Brooks/ Cole.

2-5   THE IMPACT OF AGENCY POLICY ON INTERVENTION WITH A FAMILY AFFECTED BY ATTENTION-DEFICIT HYPERACTIVITY DISORDER AND/OR OPPOSITIONAL DEFIANT DISORDER

Introduction

This case illustrates the ways in which organizational requirements may impact intervention at the client level. Financial considerations at this agency sometimes supersede the best interests of the client in formulating treatment plans. In this instance, a child and his family have established a positive working relationship with a social worker. The social worker increases contact with the family based on a need to increase billable client hours and then diminishes contact when this financial requirement no longer is necessary. The child and family experience a loss and are angry over the change. The case scenario offers an opportunity to consider, in depth, ethical dilemmas that social workers face between organizational expectations and responsibility to clients. Furthermore, there may be special factors for students to think about in this situation, pertaining specifically to the needs of clients diagnosed with ADHD/ODD, based on recommended practice strategies. Students can explore and discuss interventions at the individual, family, and programmatic levels. Students practice organizational change scenarios. The case can also be used to learn about appropriate client transfer and management of home-based services. Theoretical frameworks include developmental theory, ecosystems theory, family systems, and organizational theory.

Case Study

A private agency that provides home-based services for severely emotionally disturbed children has a contract with the county mental health agency. Funds disbursed by the county must be utilized, and the program must be running at full capacity in order for the agency to continue receiving funds for the program. County mental health provides all of the referrals to the home-based services agency.

Agency supervisors each are responsible for five team members. Each team member is required to carry a caseload of ten to fifteen clients. The caseload needs to have a balance between high- and low-maintenance children so the team is not overloaded. The team may request or create five low-maintenance client cases. Requests are submitted to supervisors who distribute county referrals. Cases are created, in part, by requesting family interventions and the involvement of low-maintenance siblings. These low-maintenance siblings can be seen at less costly resources such as local family service agencies.

Each individual team member must bill sixty-five percent of his or her day on direct client time. In order to meet this quota, some team members will spend more time with one severely emotionally disturbed child. For example, a counselor who is low in terms of direct client contact, short of his quota for a week or month, will create a three-hour visit time period for one of his clients. This is what Joshua chose to do with the Hiller family.

Matt Hiller is a twelve-year-old youngster being raised solely by his mother, Elizabeth. Matt is attending a special school for emotionally disturbed children where he is three years educationally and emotionally behind in his age group. Furthermore, he is having constant behavioral problems. This information is well documented within his county file. In fact, a school psychologist has diagnosed Matt as having Attention-Deficit Hyperactivity Disorder (ADHD) and Oppositional Defiant Disorder (ODD). There also appears to be a history of narcotic use, spousal abuse, and child abuse by Matt's biological father.

Joshua is a social worker who has been making home visits and working with Matt for about two months. Matt is showing some improvement and has really bonded with Joshua. Matt has told Joshua that he is his best friend. Upon review of his hours of client contact, Joshua decided that he needed to spend more time with one severely emotionally disturbed child to meet his quota of billable time for direct client contact.

For a two-month period, Joshua established a routine of spending several hours with the Hiller family. He would conduct individual sessions with Matt, social skills sessions with Matt and his brother, as well as a family session with Elizabeth Hiller and her two sons. The boys liked things better when Joshua was around. Activities were more structured, and Joshua could really play basketball.

Now after two months, Joshua has re-evaluated his time commitments. Joshua's client load has increased, and he is no longer able to spend more than one hour with the Hiller family. Matt told Joshua that he doesn't care about him like he used to. He asked Joshua if he doesn't like him anymore. Ms. Hiller is very upset because the children's behaviors have become worse than prior to Joshua's intervention. She tells Joshua, "Social services always make things worse for me. You young people are always telling me how to do my stuff differently and then you make things worse. Don't ever come back to my house, ever! You understand me!" Joshua is at a loss; things had been going so well.

Everybody on the team pads their hours here or there, and Joshua's supervisor is not against this practice. Joshua decides to bring the issue of Ms. Hiller and her sons to his supervisor. They agree that maybe a new face would be able to re-establish a relationship with Ms. Hiller and her family. They decide to send you to the Hiller residence.

LEARNING OBJECTIVES

1. Analyze and explain the positive and negative impact of agency financial practices on clients and reconcile client needs with agency requirements.

2. Develop strategies for resolving ethical dilemmas involving client needs and organizational expectations.

3. Gain knowledge and comprehension of children's mental health services, learn to critique a program based on the perspective of vulnerable life conditions, and develop a program based on research and theory.

4. Develop an intervention plan for a child with ADHD/ODD that is family-oriented and based on a theoretical perspective.

5. Demonstrate knowledge and skill in home-based interventions.

6. Demonstrate skill in transferring and receiving clients.

ACTIVITIES

1. You are concerned about the policy that requires that you reach a quota of client contact hours in order to support the agency's effort to meet expectations of the funding source. If you do not join this effort, you know that the agency is in danger of losing much-needed funds. On the other hand, if you suddenly increase client contact hours, it may disrupt an established intervention plan and cause harm to the client.

   a. Divide the class into groups of six students. Each group will form two subgroups. One subgroup will defend the practice of increasing hours. The other subgroup will oppose the practice.
   b. Discuss ways of reconciling the two positions. What organizational and community interventions might you use to resolve the dilemma?
   c. Convene a mock staff meeting. Take a leadership role in the group in advocating for an organizational policy change. Demonstrate how you would deal with opposition to your recommendation.

2. You are the social worker taking over for Joshua. In your small group, discuss the approach you would take to make the transition with this family. Using role-play, demonstrate how you would carry out this plan with the mother, family, and Matt.

3. Given Matt's diagnosis of ADHD, and based on current knowledge and research, discuss in your group which interventions are most appropriate for him and his family. In light of his diagnosis and history, explain his and his family reactions to the shifts in Joshua's contact hours.

4. In your group, describe the services for children with ADHD in your community. What is your assessment of their adequacy? Develop a group consensus on what would be the ideal configuration of services for this population.

SUGGESTED READINGS

American Academy of Pediatrics. (2000). *Diagnosis and evaluation of the child with attention-deficit/ hyperactivity disorder* (AC0002). Available: www.aap.org/policy/ac0002.html.

Carrey, N. (1999). Making the grade. *Readings: A Journal of Reviews and Commentary in Mental Health, 14:1,* 6–12.

Congress, E., and Gummer, B. (1997). Is the Code of Ethics as applicable to agency executives as it is to direct service practitioners? In E. Gambrill (Ed.), *Controversial issues in social work ethics, values, and obligations* (pp. 137–143). Boston: Allyn & Bacon.

Grandpre, R. (1998). *Ritalin nation: Rapid-fire culture and its transformation of human consciousness.* New York: Norton.

Johnson, H. (1988). Drugs, dialogue, or diet: Diagnosing and treating the hyperactive child. *Social Work, 33,* 349–355.

YOUTH AND VIOLENCE

INTRODUCTION

The four case studies in this chapter deal with current problems of adolescent youth exposed to violence. Timely topics of teen pregnancy, homeless youth, school violence, and youth in the criminal justice system are addressed. All of the cases provide an opportunity for students to increase their understanding of the relationship among community, family, and interpersonal violence. Students are exposed to a variety of interventions including behavior modification, outreach, case management, program development, conflict resolution, and community organization.

In Cases 3-1 and 3-2, students shift from a focus on an individual to a focus on a population as they consider ways to develop prevention programs to address teen pregnancy and abuse by foster parents and stepparents. In developing a community response to school violence (Case 3-3), students practice strategic skills as they create solutions that address and balance the concerns of multiple constituencies. They become aware of how individuals and families are affected by institutional policies and how decisions at times may be made to meet the needs of an institution rather than an individual.

Incarcerated youth frequently have multiple needs and challenges including pregnancy, drug abuse, emotional problems, disrupted family relationships, gang membership, abuse, and lack of education. Case 3-4 provides insight into the problems that cause youth to be incarcerated and which must continue to be addressed when they are released. The case focuses on the structural problem of lack of access to employment due to stigma and discrimination and provides activities to engage students in planning for social change regarding employment for ex-inmates.

3-1 A SCHOOL-BASED PROGRAM FOR TEEN PARENTS

Introduction

School-based programs for teen parents allow them to continue schooling while receiving an array of services to assist them in managing their responsibilities as parents and to complete the developmental tasks of adolescence. The program described in this case study is a milieu program where staff become closely involved with students on a day-to-day basis. Many of the female teens are in exploitive and abusive relationships. This young woman's situation is typical of teens in the school program. Students apply developmental theory, ecosystems theory, the strengths perspective, and the risk and resilience model to the case. Levels of intervention addressed include individual, organizational/programmatic, and community. Students analyze the causes and consequences of two social problems—violence and teen pregnancy—as well as the relationship between interpersonal and community violence.

Case Study

Stay in School (SIS) is a special program for teenage mothers and fathers designed to encourage them to complete high school. Funding is provided by the State Department of Social Services through its Teen program and administered by a local women's center. SIS is a voluntary program and does not require that families receive public assistance. The program provides case management; one visit per month face-to-face is required. Generally BSW-level social workers are employed, each managing a caseload of forty clients. Many Teen program employees move to county child welfare positions for greater pay since a masters degree is not required, therefore, there is significant turnover. There are only two supervisors remaining as state funds have been insufficient to retain qualified caseworkers.

At the school, a milieu approach is used by the SIS program, with teachers, social workers, and counseling staff providing onsite interventions as needed on a daily basis. Increasingly in this school district, users of this program are at poverty level, seventy-two percent of whom now receive lunch free or at reduced cost. Fifteen years ago, the number of free lunch program participants in this school district was about twenty percent. In recent years at the school, there has been an increase in the pregnancy rate for fourteen and fifteen year olds. At the same time, the age of the fathers has increased, averaging three to ten years older than the teenage mothers.

Teens who are in welfare-reliant family systems are encouraged to attend school with financial bonuses for completing satisfactory work and potential fines for nonattendance. Program regulations require that teens be in school or they will lose $50 four times per year if work is not satisfactory. The bonus is $100 four times per year if the teenager completes satisfactory work. Some teenage mothers attend the program for a while to gain much need resources—food, clothes, and blankets. However, they may not stay long enough to get a complete high school education. Many of the students who come into the program are on the fringes of society, having slipped through the gaps in social services. Students are now coming to SIS with fewer high school credits and are reporting a higher percentage of immediate family members who are incarcerated.

Cynthia entered the program as a sophomore with a very sporadic academic history, poor attendance, and few academic credits. She is a Caucasian youth, fifteen years of age, and is described by teachers as quiet and sweet. Her boyfriend, Rigoberto, a nineteen-year-old man from Guatemala, came in with her one day and asked to enroll in the program. Staff believed Rigoberto wanted to be in close contact with Cynthia so that he could control her. He was extremely jealous, abusive, and very manipulative. Rigoberto was a gang member involved in drug dealing. He openly had sexual contacts with several other young teenage girls both inside and outside the program.

One month after delivering her first child, Cynthia became pregnant again. She continued in the program during her second pregnancy. Other teens in the program reported to the school staff that they were very concerned about her because of the severe abuse she was experiencing. When asked about the abuse, Cynthia would become defensive, apologetic, and would minimize the abuse and blame herself. She defended her boyfriend, who placated her with gifts. Cynthia returned to the program one month after delivering the second baby. Rigoberto again attempted to enroll but was not accepted due to his lack of seriousness about attending school. He continued to check up on her constantly and often appeared to be on drugs, but then stopped coming to school. Cynthia has come to school with visible signs of physical abuse such as black eyes and lacerations on her face. She recently was able to acknowledge the abuse.

There is a history of abuse in Cynthia's family. Both her mother and her sister were physically abused by her sister's father. Cynthia has never known her own father. Her mother, Laura, who has successfully completed rehabilitation for her drug use and past abuse, has been trying to be supportive to her daughter. She helped Cynthia contact the district attorney's office to get a restraining order, however, it was never served.

Rigoberto recently contacted the school staff again, asking for help and professing his love for his children and their mother. Social work staff has become very wary of his requests, as he has never followed through. They have confronted him with his abusive behavior and his avoidance of help. A Child Protective Services (CPS) worker assigned to the case told Cynthia that if she could not keep herself safe then she would lose her children. Cynthia is aware of the choice she must make and stated she would leave him for her children. She has a restraining order in her possession, which she has not signed.

LEARNING OBJECTIVES

1. Move from a client-focused problem to prevention on behalf of a population.

2. Enhance knowledge and understanding of the relationship between teen pregnancy and violence.

3. Identify and discuss biopsychosocial factors in a complex case and design a multi-level intervention plan.

4. Enhance knowledge and skill in program development, and generate program alternatives based on case study material.

ACTIVITIES

1. From a biopsychosocial and strengths perspective, what is your assessment of this situation?

2. What would a comprehensive intervention plan for Cynthia look like? Taking into account her developmental stage, what modalities and resources would you use to assist her? Who else in the client's network might you involve?

3. Based on the information in the case and the implied program goals, analyze the SIS program critically, identifying strengths and possible areas for improvement. Would you recommend any changes?

4. How would you describe the relationship between violence and teen pregnancy suggested by this case? Based on your reading and other course material, are there any community or family programs you would consider developing to reduce the incidence of violence-related teen pregnancy?

SUGGESTED READINGS

Donaldson, P., Whalen, M., and Anastas, J. (1989). Teen pregnancy and sexual abuse: Exploring the connection. *Smith College Studies in Social Work, 59,* 289–300.

Fischer, F. (1997). Evaluating the delivery of a teen pregnancy and parenting program across two settings. *Research on Social Work Practice, 7,* 350–369.

Franklin, C., and Corcoran, J. (2000). Preventing adolescent pregnancy: A review of programs and practices. *Social Work, 45,* 40–52.

3-2   OUTREACH TO HOMELESS YOUTH AT RISK

Introduction

Homeless youth pose significant challenges to social workers because they may be elusive and difficult to engage. Outreach work on the street requires special knowledge about life on the streets and skill in relationship building. The case study portrays the role of a social worker who must leave the domain of the agency and conduct case finding and follow-up on the street. The worker must tread lightly and vigilantly navigate the dangers of the street. The worker is introduced to a new homeless girl by other teenagers who have come to know and trust him. The girl's history of abuse in her family and more recently in her foster family is not an unfamiliar scenario among homeless young girls. Students consider ways of engaging this youth and crisis intervention as a strategy to provide her immediate assistance. They also become familiar with the challenges and frustrations of working in an environment where ongoing intervention and follow-up do not occur on a regular basis. Interventions include crisis intervention with an individual youth, "milieu" work on the street, and consideration of prevention of abuse in stepfamilies and foster care. Discussion can revolve around needs and services for homeless youth. Legal and ethical issues pertaining to abused youth are present. Applicable theories and frameworks are attachment theory, crisis intervention, strengths perspective, harm reduction, developmental theory, trauma theory, case management, and feminist theory.

Case Study

Skip is a case manager at a shelter for homeless, runaway, and high-risk youth. Most of the clients live on the streets. On this particular night, the outreach team is shorthanded, and, because he is an established outreach worker, he joined the three-person team. It is a cold night, and there are more drug dealers, pimps, and other "predators" out on the streets tonight, who make a living from exploiting youth.

Skip knows he is being watched. It is late and he has already seen enough for one night, but he stays, waiting for the chance to talk to one more youth. As he lingers, two girls and an eleven-year-old boy disappear into several passing cars as they work their nightly job as sex workers, selling their bodies for a safe place to sleep or the various "medications" that help ease some of the pain from life on the streets.

As he leaves an abandoned building or "squat" (a street person's motel), he is approached by a small group of teens wearing ragged, dirty clothing. It is very dark, but he can tell some of them had obviously been "using" by their behavior. It is likely that most of the members of this group are "packing" some kind of protection such as knives and chains. None of the teens observed are smiling or talking.

Many thoughts run through his mind. Suddenly, the leader (the most cocky one) says "Let's kill them!" but then one of them calls Skip by name and they all start laughing. He is relieved because he recognizes them as "his kids" and greets them with handshakes and hugs while giving out food, condoms, and personal greetings.

Mike approaches Skip and pulls him aside. He has a girl, Rhonda, with him that Skip has never seen before, and he makes a visual assessment of her. Mike says to Rhonda, "This is the guy I have been telling you about. He is not like the other social workers; he listens, and he will try to help you out."

Rhonda is Caucasian and approximately fourteen years old. She has circular burn marks on her right forearm. She is wearing clean clothes and sticks out like a sore thumb. As Skip talks to her, it is obvious that she is very scared, lacks street smarts, and would be lucky to survive more than one week on these streets. Rhonda tells Skip that after she had been raped repeatedly by her step-dad, and her mom didn't care enough about Rhonda-to stop him, she was placed in foster care. Within a week of her foster placement, Rhonda was molested by her foster father. After three months, Rhonda ran away from her foster family. Parts of Rhonda's story are missing because she has blocked them out. She cries and wonders why she hasn't killed herself yet.

Skip engages Rhonda, telling her that he is glad that she is alive, is out of the abusive family environments, and compliments her on doing what she had to in order to survive. He invites her to the drop-in center for a hot meal and a chance to pick up some clothes and personal hygiene supplies. (He avoids using the word "shelter" because of legal technicalities of harboring a runaway.) He reassures Rhonda that she does not have to stay at the drop-in center. He invites the teens as a group. Rhonda declines his offer, but Mike says that he will bring her by another time.

A week has passed and Skip has not seen Rhonda on outreach or at the shelter. The "crew" she was with said they did not know where she was either. He is getting ready to go home for the evening and, as he turns around, Rhonda is standing just outside the doorway and she is looking down. Her once clean clothes are now torn and dirty. She has multiple bruises on her face and neck.

LEARNING OBJECTIVES

1. Increase awareness and sensitivity to issues pertaining to homeless youth. Develop programmatic solutions to the problem of homeless youth.

2. Increase knowledge about the foster care system in relation to adolescents. Analyze the current status of such foster care and develop recommendations for improved service delivery for those in the system and transitioning toward independence.

3. Increase knowledge and skill in outreach interventions with vulnerable adolescents who have experienced physical and/or sexual abuse. Apply theory and research to intervention strategies.

ACTIVITIES

1. How might you assess Rhonda's immediate situation? What things should Skip be looking for in his visual assessment of Rhonda on the streets?

2. Discuss how you would intervene with Rhonda at this point given your previous contact and Rhonda's previous history. What issues would you consider in attempting to engage her?

3. Referring to the case vignette, discuss the approaches that Skip uses as an outreach worker. How does this "milieu" differ from other treatment settings, and what is the impact on your practice?

4. What ethical or legal obligations may be present in this situation?

5. Rhonda has been vulnerable as a stepchild and as a foster child. Discuss various factors in stepfamilies and in the foster care system that contribute to risk. What macro-level interventions/strategies might be employed to prevent sexual abuse in stepfamilies and physical or sexual abuse in the foster family system?

6. What services are present for homeless youth in your community? What programmatic interventions would you recommend to improve those services?

7. How does the foster care system in your community make services available to adolescents who have survived abuse or have experienced exploitation on the streets? What kinds of transitional services are available to assist youth who are moving out of foster care into independent living?

SUGGESTED READINGS

Bronstein, L. (1996). Intervening with homeless youths: Direct practice without blaming the victim. *Child and Adolescent Social Work Journal, 13,* 127–138.

Guterman, N., and Cameron, M. (1997). Assessing the impact of community violence on children and youth. *Social Work, 42,* 495–505.

Hinton-Nelson, M., Roberts, M., and Snyder, C. (1996). Early adolescents exposed to violence: Hope and vulnerability to victimization. *American Journal of Orthopsychiatry, 66,* 346–353.

National Clearinghouse on Families and Youth. (1995). *Youth with runaway, throwaway, and homeless experiences: Prevalence, drug-use, and other at-risk behaviors.* Available: www.ncfy.com.

Rotheram-Borus, M., Mahler, K., Koopman, C., and Langabeer, K. (1996). Sexual abuse history and associated multiple risk behavior in adolescent runaways. *American Journal of Orthopsychiatry, 66,* 390–400.

3.3   RESPONSE TO SCHOOL VIOLENCE: A COMMUNITY-BASED APPROACH

CHUCK GATTEN

Introduction

School violence has become a major challenge for communities across the United States. Social workers play a key role in developing constructive responses and strategies for prevention. The case here describes the efforts of a grassroots community-based organization to deal with violence in a public school district. The group is made up of parents and concerned citizens of the local community. Students are asked to develop a coherent analysis of the problem of school violence. They consider interventions that address the concerns of multiple constituencies including students, parents, the school board, school personnel, and the community. They critique the interventions used by the neighborhood organization in the case and develop their own based on theory. Interventions include group methods, prevention, organizational change, and community organization. Relevant theories are ecosystems theory, organizational theory, and conflict resolution.

Case Study

On April 16, 2002, the television newscasts and newspapers in Riverview were filled with the story that three students at Don Juan Junior High School had plotted to bomb their school. The parents attended a meeting to hear the Jefferson School Board's discussion about this latest incident of violence on one of their school campuses.

In November of the previous year, the Neighborhood Action Alliance (NAA), a grassroots organization of concerned citizens picketed the W.E.B. DuBois Junior High campus because of violence occurring there. A young girl had a gun held to her head by another student, an alleged gang member. The reaction of the school and the district superintendent was entirely unsatisfactory to NAA. They had a meeting, promised a safety plan, but to date, nothing has been accomplished to set parents' and children's minds at ease about going to school without the threat of violence. In fact, according to NAA, the district has punished the girl who was the victim, offering her no counseling support for her experience, and moving her to another school within the district against her and her mother's wishes. The mother had asked that her daughter be sent to a private school. NAA members were quite perplexed when they discovered that the student who held the gun to the girl's head was also transferred to the same school! They concluded that both students were kept in the district in order to keep the average daily attendance (A.D.A.) funds it collects on each student.

In March, the NAA received a complaint from a parent of a Rio Grande Junior High School student, again in the Jefferson School District, who was physically hit by one of her teachers. The Alliance was concerned that the teacher's behavior was not dealt with, yet the student was charged with pushing a teacher and received six months' probation. Various incidents of violence have now occurred in three of the Jefferson District's junior high schools, all within the last year.

The NAA has met with the Jefferson District Superintendent and District Board members to ask for remedy of these situations but has been dissatisfied since nothing has been done except to punish the victims of the violence. They assisted the girl threatened with the gun in obtaining a pro bono lawyer to advocate for her. They sent a letter to the editor of the local newspaper about their concerns. NAA has publicly asked, "What kind of message is being sent to the parents and students by this inept school district? Clearly, this school district doesn't know how to deal with violent situations, and in fact, is making matters worse."

LEARNING OBJECTIVES

1. Articulate a coherent analysis of violence in schools based on an ecological perspective.

2. Demonstrate advanced skill in developing a community intervention plan.

3. Apply appropriate frameworks and theories for understanding a community problem and for intervention at an institutional and community level.

ACTIVITIES

1. Do you agree with the tactics and actions that have been taken so far by the Neighborhood Action Alliance? Defend your position.

2. If you were a staff organizer for the Neighborhood Action Alliance, what would you do in addition to, or differently from the actions described in the case scenario?

3. There have been reports of school violence by pre-adolescents and adolescents in many cities in the United States. Based on your knowledge of human development and social, economic, familial, and emotional factors, present a coherent explanation of the various possible underlying or contributing factors to this behavior.

4. Based on your understanding of school violence, if you were a school social worker in the Jefferson district, how do you think school violence issues should be handled? Consider the differences in the school's perspective and the vantage points of the parents and students.

5. What theories and perspectives are you using to guide your responses to the questions in this exercise?

SUGGESTED READINGS

Alinsky, S. (1971). *Rules for radicals* (Chapters 1 & 2). New York: Vintage Books.

Astor, R. (1998). School social workers and school violence: Personal safety, training, and violence programs. *Social Work, 43,* 193–288.

Bobo, K., Kendall, J., and Max, S. (1991). *Organizing for social change.* Santa Ana, CA: Seven Locks Press.

Brager, G., Specht, H., and Torezyner, J. (1987). *Community organizing* (2nd ed.). New York: Columbia University Press.

Kahn, S. (1994). *How people get power.* Washington, DC: NASW Press.

3-4 COMMUNITY-BASED SERVICES FOR YOUTH RELEASED ON PAROLE

Introduction

This case study illustrates a typical example of an adolescent who has been involved with the juvenile justice system. The case history includes multiple issues for study: abuse, drug use, criminal activity, gang membership, mental illness, and teen pregnancy. For students, the key issues are to gain an understanding of the parole system, the follow-up service delivery system for youth who have been released from prison, and to assess gaps in services and resources. Among those is the need to develop employment opportunities so that the young person can gain financial independence in order to get back on his or her feet. Employment discrimination is one of the stressors that many ex-prisoners must deal with. Due to multiple needs of the client, case management is a primary intervention for study. Relevant theories are risk and resilience, strengths perspective, cognitive-behavioral approach, and trauma theory. Multilevel interventions considered include case management, individual counseling, population-based prevention strategies, and program development. Racial and gender issues can be examined in this case as well.

Case Study

Eva is a twenty-year-old African American woman. She was sent to the State Youth Correctional Services for two years due to theft and prostitution to support her drug and alcohol addiction. Eva appeared before the Youth Parole Board (YPB) for a Parole Consideration Hearing. After being released to the residence of her aunt and uncle, Eva reported to the parole office a week later and was assigned to Susan, a social work intern.

Eva has one older brother and one older half sister. Eva's father has been absent since she was two years old. He was abusive to Eva, her mother, and her older sister. He is currently serving a life sentence in a state prison. Both parents have a history of drug abuse that was ongoing at the time of Eva's birth and early childhood. Eva was raised by her mother and grandmother. She was very close to her grandmother, who died ten years prior. Her behavior problems started after her grandmother's death. She joined a gang and began using drugs and alcohol at that time. At age fifteen, she moved in with John, a boyfriend who was ten years her senior. Eva has had two pregnancies, both with John. Both infants were drug-exposed and died shortly after birth. John was physically abusive to Eva. He beat her and forced her to sell fake drugs for which she has been shot and stabbed. Eva has a history of violent behavior. She has several prior offenses involving assault and has received disciplinary action due to her outbursts while incarcerated.

During Susan's first contact with Eva, Eva's demeanor was attentive. She asked many questions, which indicated that she understood the conditions as explained. They reviewed together the special conditions of parole mandated by the Youth Parole Board. They discussed parole expectations and services available to parolees.

Eva's goals include gaining employment and passing the GED high school equivalency examination. She is concerned about the challenges in finding work as a parolee. Eva has also tested as a special education student, indicating that she is functioning below others her age. Finally, Eva is concerned that she not cause economic hardship to her aunt and uncle while living in their home. Eva is also concerned that, currently without health insurance, she has been released with a three-day supply of medication for depression and hallucinations. In the past, when Eva has not taken the medication, she has, at times, acted in a paranoid and violent manner. According to corrections staff, Eva made great strides this year in managing her anger.

Most of Eva's former friends have gang affiliations and are likely current drug users. She largely associates friendship with drugs and criminal behavior and is afraid of getting into trouble again. Eva wants to and is mandated by the Youth Parole Board to form new relationships with positive peers.

Susan and Eva have begun to discuss means for Eva to establish her independence. These include getting access to medical assistance, continuing education at the juvenile court high school, and looking for employment. Eva has responded favorably. However, she is concerned about getting new work and creating new friends. She does not believe that Susan can help her in these two areas. She feels stigmatized by her history of juvenile incarceration as well as by her history of drug and alcohol use. She is most concerned that employers have access to the juvenile criminal records of potential employees unless the records are sealed. She expresses tremendous feelings of guilt, shame, and sorrow over the loss of her children. At times she thinks about reuniting with John but is now uncertain about that relationship.

LEARNING OBJECTIVES

1. Acquire knowledge of correctional services for youth and special issues such as employment and/or rehabilitation facing youth who have been incarcerated.

2. Develop a program for paroled youth based on service delivery gaps and community support.

3. Explain the interface between gang affiliation, drugs, and criminal behavior, and apply methods of prevention to these problem areas.

4. Develop a multilevel intervention plan, including case management for a paroled youth, that addresses multiple needs and problems.

ACTIVITIES

1. Base your answers to the following on an empowerment and strengths perspective.

   a. Discuss the interconnection between Eva's psychological and physical development, her family history, and her community/neighborhood experience. How do these factors explain her current situation and the possible prognosis?

   b. Develop an intervention plan for Eva, and describe how it is related to the assessment in part a. Would you involve Eva's aunt and uncle in your intervention plan? If so, what family approaches might you use to involve them?

   c. What services would you provide for Eva, and how would you coordinate them?

   d. What kinds of preventive programs/interventions would you recommend at the family and community levels in order to prevent juvenile criminal behavior?

2. Using role-play, demonstrate your second interview with Eva in which you attempt to engage her and address the concerns she expressed during the initial interview.

3. People who have been incarcerated frequently have difficulty in finding employment.

   a. How would you conduct yourself in the role of advocate for Eva to help her secure employment?

   b. How might you go about being a change agent, develop community awareness about the problem, and bring about changes that would improve employment opportunities? How might you involve employers in providing jobs to ex-prisoners? Present your step-by-step approach to the group.

SUGGESTED READINGS

Alexander, R. (2000). *Counseling, treatment, and intervention methods with juvenile and adult offenders.* Belmont, CA: Wadsworth.

Armstrong, T. (1991). *Intensive intervention with high-risk youths: Promising approaches in juvenile probation and parole.* Monsey, NY: Criminal Justice Press.

Gutierrez, L., Parsons, R., and Cox, E. (1998). *Empowerment in social work practice.* Pacific Grove, CA: Brooks/Cole.

Lemmon, J. (1999). A pragmatic approach to parole aftercare: Evaluation of a community reintegration program for high-risk youthful offenders. *Juvenile Justice Update, 5,* 10.

Molidor, C. (1996). Female gang members: A profile of aggression and victimization. *Social Work, 41,* 251–257.

Saleeby, D. (2002). *The strengths perspective in social work practice.* Boston, MA: Allyn & Bacon.

Tonn, R. (1999). Turning the tables: The Safer foundation's youth empowerment program. *Corrections Today, 61,* 76–78.

CHAPTER FOUR

FAMILY AND COMMUNITY INTERVENTIONS TO ADDRESS VIOLENCE AND TRAUMA IN ADULTS

4-1 Multilevel Solutions to Violence with an African American Family using Oppression and Feminist Theories

4-2 A Cambodian Woman with Severe Psychological and Social Trauma

4-3 Saving *STOP:* A Community-Based Program to Reduce Jail Recidivism among the Mentally Ill

INTRODUCTION

The three case scenarios in this chapter address various aspects of interpersonal violence and community violence and their interconnections. The cases cover structural levels of violence including community violence; gender, racial, and workplace oppression; and organizational conflict. In Case 4-1, stressors due to interpersonal and community violence and gender and racial issues affect the client and her family. The case illustrates the way in which the workplace is part of the client's ecosystem and can both reflect and affect coping capacity. Case 4-2 graphically describes the effects of multiple traumas due to war, displacement, and family violence on the emotional and physical state of an adult woman. It provides an excellent example of post-traumatic stress syndrome. Organizational issues are highlighted in Case 4-3, which is about a program at risk of being abolished, partly due to conflicts between the two agencies responsible for its implementation. Strategies for organizational and community intervention are studied. Students then move from the organizational issues to the client level where the impact of the organizational conflict on a client's treatment is illustrated. The case provides an opportunity to delve into the topic of the interface between mental illness and the correctional system. The ethnic backgrounds of the clients are African American and Cambodian, thus giving students an opportunity to enhance their knowledge of working with these cultures. Interventions include individual,

45

group, organizational, community, and program development. Theories include ecosystems, feminist, oppression, constructivist, trauma, and organizational.

4-1 MULTILEVEL SOLUTIONS TO VIOLENCE WITH AN AFRICAN AMERICAN FAMILY USING OPPRESSION AND FEMINIST THEORIES

Introduction

This case study depicts the interactions among social oppression, interpersonal violence, and personal stress. The client's distress is exhibited in the workplace through poor performance and inability to concentrate on her work. The case offers an opportunity for students to critically examine the impact of oppression among African Americans as a group on their family relationships. The client, a single mother recently separated from her husband, is struggling to manage her inadequate financial situation with job and parenting responsibilities. Gender role factors also contribute to the client's oppression and provide an opportunity to apply feminist theory to gain an understanding of the case dynamics as well as to develop an intervention plan. The case lends itself to consideration of individual, organizational, and community interventions to deal with oppression and violence.

Case Study

Estelle, thirty-six, is an African American woman with three children. Her husband, Jim, from whom she has been separated for one year, worked in the steel mills for twelve years until three years ago, when he was laid off due to the closing of the mills. Jim had difficulty becoming re-employed, started drinking heavily, and then became increasingly violent. On three occasions her daughter witnessed violence between Estelle and her husband. After Estelle and Jim separated, he left the state to look for work. They have a legal separation that specifies child support payments of $600, yet he has not made child support payments even though he has found work. Estelle has not been successful in getting the State's Attorney's office to enforce the child support agreement.

Estelle works as an administrative assistant at the county court. Estelle began to experience panic attacks about six months ago. She also appeared to be quite depressed. She has been absent from work, has trouble concentrating on her job, and has withdrawn from contacts with colleagues. In part, her absenteeism is due to her extreme concern about her children when she is not at home. At work she constantly telephones home to make sure they are alright. She has requested overtime work so that she could improve her financial situation, but she has not been assigned any extra work due to her poor performance. Her male supervisor called her in and told her she was at risk of losing her job if she did not improve her performance. She contacted the mental health managed care program offered under her health benefits plan. She has been assigned to you for evaluation.

A psychiatric evaluation revealed that Estelle had experienced an episode of panic attacks and depression when she was thirteen years old. She was seen by her family doctor and was given anti-anxiety medications. She also had experienced an episode of depression during her early twenties. Currently, she states she generally has feelings of hopelessness, has lost her appetite, is sleeping more than she has in the past, and has no energy to do anything. Since her husband left, she has had no social contacts and is extremely isolated. She rarely leaves the house except to go to work.

Estelle reported that both her mother and sister had experienced depression and panic attacks. She had witnessed her father's violent outbursts toward her mother. He had a severe drinking problem. Estelle now lives in a community where there is increasing gang and drug activity and gun violence. She worries constantly about the safety of her children. Her twelve-year-old daughter and ten-year-old son stay with her mother most days after school, but sometimes her mother is unable to care for them because she has severe arthritis and is often in pain. Her sixteen-year-old son needs greater supervision as he has recently engaged in petty theft and has been hanging out with friends who sell drugs. Estelle has found that she is unable to enforce a curfew, and her son recently stayed out all night. She frequently gets into arguments with her mother over the best way to discipline her children.

Estelle, who in the past has been an excellent worker, is embarrassed by her recent poor performance. Her supervisor has made it more difficult by criticizing her in front of her co-workers. He is unsympathetic to her concerns about her family and cannot understand the drastic change in her mood and behavior. This adds to her lack of desire to go to work.

LEARNING OBJECTIVES

1. Apply oppression theory and feminist theory at multiple levels of intervention.

2. Starting with the individual as the unit of attention, coherently articulate the impact of contextual factors on the case situation.

3. Design a multilevel intervention plan to deal with oppression and violence.

ACTIVITIES

1. Discuss the stressors present in Estelle's life and her coping responses.

2. Discuss your differential diagnosis of Estelle. Explain the process you went through to arrive at it.

3. GlenMaye, in her article "Empowerment of Women," explores alienation of self, the double bind of women, and institutional sexism as conditions that describe

the context of women in our culture. How are these concepts evident in Estelle's case?

4. Several authors (e.g., Van Soest) emphasize the importance of considering the context of oppression as critical in the conceptualization of treatment for depression in women. What does that mean, and how would consideration of powerlessness, isolation, institutional sexism, and pervasive stress help inform your multilevel intervention?

5. How would the information in questions 1 through 4 help you design an intervention plan? What would the components of your intervention plan look like at the individual, institutional, and structural/cultural levels of violence in Estelle's life?

SUGGESTED READINGS

GlenMaye, L. (1998). Empowerment of women. In L. Gutierrez, R. Parsons, and E. Cox, *Empowerment in social work practice: A source book* (pp. 29–51). Pacific Grove, CA: Brooks/Cole.

Harrell, S. (2000). A multidimensional conceptualization of racism-related stress: Implications for the well being of people of color. *American Journal of Orthopsychiatry, 70,* 42–57.

Sachs, J., and Newdom, F. (1999). *Clinical work and social action: An integrative approach.* Binghamton, NY: Haworth Press.

Swenson, C. (1998). Clinical social work's contribution to a social justice perspective. *Social Work, 43,* 527–537.

Van Soest, D. (1997). *The global crisis of violence: Common problems, universal causes, shared solutions.* Washington, DC: NASW Press.

4-2   A CAMBODIAN WOMAN WITH SEVERE PSYCHOLOGICAL AND SOCIAL TRAUMA

JUAN HERNANDEZ

Introduction

Cambodian refugees to the United States represent a group with special needs and experiences related to their precipitous and involuntary displacement from their country due to war. This case study illustrates the impact of multiple levels of severe trauma and violence on individual emotional and physical functioning. The effects of war are vividly depicted. The client has witnessed numerous atrocities as well as the annihilation of several family members. Interpersonal violence related to social oppression as well as gender is described. Yet there is strong evidence of successful coping and survival abilities displayed by the client. Students struggle with gaining an understanding of cultural dynamics in assessing medical symptoms and in comprehending the illness behavior of the client. They consider individual and group approaches for this population as well as advocacy and social change interventions. Students also study and critique the service delivery system for Southeast Asian immigrants as well as the impact of current legislation. Constructivist theory, trauma theory, empowerment theory, feminist theory, and the strengths perspective are applicable to this case.

Case Study

Lily Phim is a fifty-five-year-old Cambodian woman who left Cambodia fifteen years ago. She came to the United States seven years ago. She lives in Midsize City with two of her ten children: a son, age sixteen, and a daughter, age eleven. Also in the household are employed adults—a married couple and two brothers. Three children reside in Cambodia, two are in Arizona, one is in the U.S. Navy, and two died in Cambodia. The address is a single-family dwelling situated in a middle-class neighborhood. The residence was well maintained. Present during this assessment interview were Ms. Phim, her friend who visits her weekly, and Mr. Tran, a highly experienced interpreter.

Ms. Phim was thin and had a drawn face. Her most prominent complaints were headaches with head numbness and chest pain. She reported that the pain began five years ago while she resided in another state. The pain is in her temples and along the sides of her head and sometimes involves her whole head. She experiences the pain at intervals of two or three days. Each episode will last a whole day and proceed into the night, causing her sleep to become disturbed. It was determined that what she calls "head numbness" really refers to the intensity of the pain. Sometimes other senses such as hearing are obliterated. She has chest pain near her right shoulder whenever she carries anything. When she has this pain, she finds it difficult to breathe. Ms. Phim showed the interviewer how she jumps up and down to relieve the pain. This condition began about twenty years ago.

She revealed the possible cause of her head and chest pains as the result of frequently being beaten with a board by both her first and second husbands. She had suffered a fractured skull and other injuries from those beatings. She stated that she preferred not discussing these things. X-Rays had been taken of her head but she did not know the results. Ms. Phim's doctor has prescribed four or five medications that she states are ineffective; but since she threw away the containers after she ran out of them, it was not possible to determine what they were.

Ms. Phim said that she suffers from these symptoms, as well as dizziness and tiredness, whenever she thinks about her life and the terrible losses that she has had. She recalled how her sister, while enslaved by the Khmer Rouge, witnessed many atrocities, suffered a heart attack during that ordeal, and died within hours of the attack. She mentioned that her mother died when Ms. Phim was young; her father died more recently. She also lost two brothers, a sister, two brothers-in-law, and two sisters-in-law, in addition to two of her own children. Some of her children were separated from her and sent to a separate labor camp. She is worried that her son who is in the Navy might be sent overseas and be killed. She wept as she recounted these events and stated such suffering was a private matter that she did not wish to discuss further. Records indicate that she witnessed the torture and execution of her first husband in Cambodia.

Ms. Phim is quite articulate and personable, yet she is anxious and fidgety. As she spoke, she would wring her hands with her arms straightened so that her hands were twisted and between her knees. Her face became very drawn, her eyes welled with tears, and deep lines formed on her face as she spoke.

Her headaches began after the disappearance of her second husband. She reported that he ran off after their arrival in the United States, and that she did not know where he was. She was glad that he left. She experiences dizziness induced by any exercise or exertion. The dizzy spells may last for two or three hours.

In her homeland, Ms. Phim managed a grocery store prior to the Pol Pot regime. After the Khmer Rouge released her, she was supported through communal farming. She left Cambodia, was encamped in Thailand for eight years, and then was settled in New York where she worked for one month for a sewing company. She relocated to Midsize City three years ago.

Ms. Phim and her two children receive Temporary Aid to Needy Families. She is exempt from work requirements due to her medical condition. She arises early each day, about 2:00 or 3:00 A.M. and will sit in her bedroom. During the day, she mainly lies down in the bedroom or sits on the sofa in the living room. She has very little interaction with others. Her daughter prepares meals when she is home. Ms. Phim weighs ninety pounds; she eats one meal a day. She has been taking the medication of one of the other adults in the household hoping it would help her sleep but it has not worked.

LEARNING OBJECTIVES

1. Identify and understand the relationship between and consequences of severe psychological and social trauma.

2. Demonstrate an ability to incorporate cultural knowledge into an assessment and intervention plan.

3. Apply the strengths and empowerment perspectives.

4. Learn about service delivery to the Cambodian/Southeast Asian population.

5. Understand the impact of the current political/legislative environment on the immigrant/refugee.

ACTIVITIES

1. Discuss the relative influence of psychological, biological/physical, and sociocultural factors in this case and how they would affect your assessment. Consider the impact of multiple levels of trauma. Describe Ms. Phim's strengths and incorporate them into your assessment.

2. What would be the most effective types of interventions for Ms. Phim based on your assessment?

3. What theoretical frameworks would be most helpful in explaining your assessment and in choosing interventions?

4. Assuming this woman lived in your community, what culturally appropriate medical and mental health resources would be available to her? Identify any gaps in services and what role you might play in alleviating them.

5. Applying the strengths perspective, in small groups, role-play an interview with Ms. Phim to determine what she might want or need to improve her situation. Assuming you are of a different cultural background from Ms. Phim, how would you address cultural differences? If you were of the same culture, how would you approach her?

6. As a refugee, what federal and state laws have an impact on Ms. Phim's life and her ability to obtain services? As a social worker who has a responsibility to promote social justice, how would you go about advocating for changes that would improve the lives of refugees.

REFERENCE

Nicholson, B., and Kay, D. (1999). Group treatment of traumatized Cambodian women: A culture-specific approach. *Social Work, 44,* 470–479.

4-3   SAVING *STOP:* A COMMUNITY-BASED PROGRAM TO REDUCE JAIL RECIDIVISM AMONG THE MENTALLY ILL

Introduction

The following case vignette describes an innovative program based on a new partnership between mental health services and local correctional institutions, which is designed to divert mentally ill offenders from jail, provide services to those who become incarcerated, and to ensure follow-up for those who are released. The services that have been successful are threatened with reduced funding, a situation partly a result of interorganizational differences. The vignette illustrates how organizational conflict and inappropriate care can be detrimental to an individual inmate. Students critically analyze the interorganizational relationships using a systems perspective and develop strategies for organizational change to benefit clients based on social work ethics and values. Using advocacy skills, students develop a strategy for restoring funding to save the program. Interventions include advocacy, public testimony, organizational change, and multilevel treatment planning. Theoretical frameworks include organizational theory, systems theory, conflict resolution, and empowerment theory.

Case Study

In 1994, the Stay Out of Prison (STOP) program was started in Coronado County, California, to provide assessment and treatment to persons with mental illness who were incarcerated in increasing numbers in the county jail for misdemeanors. The increase in incarcerations was associated with the decrease in local community-based mental health services. Up until that point the forensic program was focused on persons who committed felonies and did not provide special services to the mentally ill. STOP was initiated by the Department of Human Services, of which Mental Health was a subsection. It was implemented collaboratively with the Sheriff's Department and functioned as a partnership between the jail and the Department of Mental Health. Social workers were hired by the county to conduct assessments, to recommend treatment during incarceration, and to develop a follow-up plan to be implemented upon release. By statute the jail was required to provide medical treatment to incarcerated persons comparable to what they would receive outside of jail. Under the new program, the sheriff provided space, some social work positions, oversaw a suicide watch program in the jail, and was responsible for medical care including psychiatric medication. The STOP program was, for the most part, under the auspices of the mental health department, except for suicide watch, which was under the jurisdiction of the jail, as they had round-the-clock staff.

The purpose of STOP was to assess people within twenty-four hours and before adjudication. Prior to STOP, a nurse conducted a preliminary screening for history of medical and mental health problems. If the inmate said he or she had no history, usually there was no further investigation. Under the new program, a social worker from STOP would conduct a thorough assessment and could then make recommendations at the court hearing that might divert the person from a jail sentence. Diversion had been taking place for a long time. The STOP program received additional funding to enhance the program and was supported by the sheriff because it would free up beds in the jail. A major benefit to the inmates was that they could get a reduced sentence or be released on probation. The STOP treatment conditions were tied to probation. An important goal was to prevent recidivism. STOP provided case management so that an array of services could be accessed by the client.

For people not deemed suitable for release, the goal of the program was to provide appropriate mental health care during the jail stay and, through proper follow-up, prevent recidivism. Department of Mental Health psychiatrists provided part-time psychiatric services to the jail in order to ensure accurate diagnoses and necessary medication. Initially, the county was pleased to have resources to provide services to this segment of its jail population. In the first several months, the program demonstrated significant success. Inmates received medication, thus making their behavior more manageable and the environment more harmonious for other inmates. Social workers were available to provide weekly sessions with clients, more if necessary. Excellent relationships were developed with the county mental health services so that a continuum of a care could be provided upon release.

The Sheriff's Department became uncomfortable with the costliness of the program, as it was not used to allocating funds for mental illness care. While there was interest in diversion and in preventing recidivism, the overall philosophy of the jail was punishment, not care and rehabilitation. Contacts by residents with the social worker were seen as counterproductive to the goals of the jail. Jail administrators began various efforts to reduce the cost of the program. They hired their own physician to prescribe medication and to review psychiatric orders to see if lower-cost medication could be substituted. This caused increasing conflict between the Department of Mental Health and the jail. Social workers were caught in the middle of this conflict as they began to see their clients receiving less than optimal care, and, in some cases, clients deteriorated due to lack of or inappropriate medication.

The Mental Health Department was not entirely supportive of the program since treatment of mentally ill persons who committed crimes had always been something the department had tried to avoid. Some administrators in the department believed that jail rather than diversion was appropriate for those who had committed crimes. At the time of funding renewal, there was talk of closing the program due to the excessive cost. When the proposed county budget was publicized, funds for the program had been deleted in spite of documented success in both diversion and recidivism.

Beverly Richards

Beverly Richards was admitted to jail in May 1996 after getting into a fight with her boyfriend subsequent to taking drugs and disturbing the peace at her apartment. The landlord called the police. She is a twenty-eight-year old African American woman with two children, Mike, age eight, and Lily, age three. The children were taken into care by the county. The day after the initial interview with the nurse, the STOP social worker determined that she had Major Depression secondary to drug use and a Personality Disorder. She decided Ms. Richards could benefit from treatment.

The social worker referred the client for a psychiatric evaluation so that she could start medication while awaiting adjudication. She started on Zoloft and seemed to be doing well. About a week later, the jail physician reviewed the orders and changed the medication to Elavil. Although Ms. Richards had a history of untreated depression and had no known history of suicidal behavior, she became extremely despondent over the separation from her children and her boyfriend and was experiencing symptoms due to the absence of drugs. The jail environment also had an adverse effect on her mood, as she was not used to being so isolated and without family or friends. Her admission to the jail had occurred at the time that the Sheriff was trying to tighten the budget by saving money on medication and on reducing services. Ms. Richards was found in her jail cell barely conscious after attempting suicide. The suicide watch staff had not noticed her despondency.

Shortly afterward there was a news article in the local paper reporting that a wrongful death suit had been filed by the family of another inmate who had died in jail.

LEARNING OBJECTIVES

1. Understand the relationship between organizational policies and direct services to clients.

2. Define the social work roles and develop strategies for changing organizational norms consistent with social work values.

3. Develop a political strategy to advocate for a program at the local government level. Gather and present data to support your position in a coherent manner.

4. Identify and resolve ethical dilemmas that place client needs in conflict with organizational policies.

5. Increase awareness of the interface between corrections and mental health and become sensitive to issues for clients in correctional settings.

ACTIVITIES

1. As a social worker in the STOP program, what kinds of interventions could you implement in order to save STOP?

2. Develop a one-page statement to the Board of Supervisors explaining why STOP should be continued. Choose a partner in your group and present your arguments to one another.

3. What is your assessment of the organizational situation in this case study, and what intervention plan would you propose in order to advocate for positive change? What barriers to change might you encounter, and how might you work to overcome them?

4. Based on your assessment, develop a multilevel intervention plan for Ms. Richards that uses an empowerment approach and takes into account the full range of biopsychosocial factors in this case. Include organizational and community (local and/or state level) approaches that you think might be necessary in order to fully meet this client's needs. Describe step-by-step how you would work with Ms. Richards and her client system.

5. Visit the local jail in the area in which you have your field placement and find out how services for the mentally ill are delivered. Be prepared to discuss your impressions in your group.

6. Analyze the risks that you might have to take in this setting in order to promote and maintain ethical practice. Which risks would you be willing to take, and how would you go about taking action?

SUGGESTED READINGS

Steadman, H., McCarty, J., and Morrisey, J. (1989). *The mentally ill in jail: Planning for essential services.* New York: Guilford.

■ ■ ■ ■ ■

IMMIGRANT AND REFUGEE FAMILIES

INTRODUCTION

Three immigrant families are presented in this chapter. Case 5-1 describes a Bosnian family's experience with the mental health system in the United States, as they cope with a daughter who has been hospitalized for many years due to a violent outburst when she was ten, resulting in the death of her brother. The family's coping strategies are influenced by their experiences during the war as well as cultural factors related to their ethnic background. The family appears to be middle class. Issues are raised in the case about the preparedness of the mental health providers to deliver culturally relevant services and to bridge language barriers. The case provides an excellent jumping-off point for study of mental health services to Eastern European populations.

Case 5-2 gives students insight into the process by which refugees are permitted to enter the United States. Jewish refugees have access to a well-developed service system, which is described in detail. Knowledge gained about the service delivery system can be transferred to other case situations and populations. The family in question has been admitted to the United States due to religious persecution and presents a different experience from the families who have experienced trauma due to the atrocities of war. The case provides insight into the concerns and stresses of very recent refugees. Through the specific case example, students can see how the immigration process can have an impact on individual emotional and physical health and on family dynamics.

Case 5-3 provides a contrast to Case 5-1. It depicts a Hmong family who has recently come to the United States. The head of household is a widow with limited resources and serious housing problems. Adequate services are not yet in place; therefore, students can enhance their community organization and program planning skills as they study how best to address unmet need. Differentiating between and among various Southeast Asian populations can be addressed through this case.

Special topics in this chapter include services to immigrants and refugees, the physical and emotional health of immigrants, and development of cultural competence. Interventions addressed in this chapter include individual, family, program development, and community organization. Applicable theoretical frameworks include solution-focused approach, family systems, oppression theory, and empowerment theory.

5-1 A BOSNIAN FAMILY'S STRUGGLE WITH SERIOUS MENTAL ILLNESS

Introduction

This case study focuses on the effects of trauma due to the war in Bosnia on a family that has emigrated to the United States. Students address the cultural factors that play a significant role in determining the family's coping strategies and apply family theory in order to develop a biopsychosocial assessment and treatment plan. Students apply the DSM-IV criteria to develop a diagnosis for the mentally ill client. The case raises issues about services to Eastern European clients in the mental health system. Ethical issues are also raised related to confidentiality between and among family members in a situation where a long-standing family secret is present. Two levels of intervention are considered, work with individuals and work with their families. Relevant theories are family systems, trauma theory, empowerment theory, developmental theory, and oppression theory.

Case Study

Lilja is a seventeen-year-old who has been under psychiatric care since she was age ten. She was born during the ethnic conflicts prior to the war in Bosnia and lived with her mother, her mother's sister, and her uncle. Nothing is known of her biological father. When Lilja was six years old, her mother married a Bosnian man. During the war, the family witnessed the murder and rape of several relatives and neighbors. After the war, the family lived in a Bosnian refugee camp until they emigrated to the Midwestern United States.

Lilja was raised by her aunt, whom she thought was her mother. Two more children were born to her real mother and the stepfather. Lilja was favored by the aunt, who had no children of her own, but reportedly was made to wait on and care for the other children in the household, her stepbrother and stepsister. She became increasingly angry and hostile. Lilja began to exhibit violent and assaultive behavior to the other children. When Lilja was ten years old, she became angry at her three-year-old stepbrother and pushed him down a flight of stairs. He received severe head injuries and died after being in a coma for a week. Lilja was placed in a children's mental health facility.

Since then Lilja has had a history of severe emotional outbursts and violent assaultive behavior. As an older adolescent, she frequently required seclusion and restraint to protect other patients and herself. Medication was not effective in helping to ease her symptoms, and in the past she has not been willing to participate in individual or family therapy. Lilja's mother and aunt visited often, but usually the aunt did all the talking. Often Lilja appeared to be upset and fearful after their visits, but because the aunt spoke to Lilja only in Serbo-Croatian, the staff did not know what was being said, and Lilja would not discuss these conversations with staff.

Several months ago, Lilja was moved to a new program, and the new social worker took a special interest in her. The social worker began to talk to Lilja each day from the door of her room and gradually began to develop a more trusting relationship with her. Shortly afterward, a new staff member who spoke Serbian assisted the social worker in communicating with the mother and aunt each time they came to visit. The social worker discovered that the aunt had been telling Lilja (in Serbian) to stay in seclusion as much as possible, to avoid being assaulted by male patients.

The social worker suggested that Lilja and her family meet with her to discuss safety issues and how to help Lilja. Lilja refused, but, surprisingly, the mother and aunt agreed, and this meeting became the beginning of serious family intervention. In her sessions with the mother and aunt, the worker learned that Lilja's mother had been raped as a teenager by a Serbian soldier and Lilja was born as a result. It had been decided to keep the rape a secret and simply tell people that her father had died. There was a deep family sense of shame associated with the rape. The aunt lived in constant fear that the truth might come out, or that Lilja might be raped, too. After Lilja's mother married and other children were born, Lilja's attachment to her aunt seemed to provide a solution to a shameful secret. When the family arrived in the United States, they reported that Lilja was the aunt's child and was thus listed on Lilja's immigration documents. Lilja grew up believing that her aunt was, in fact, her mother.

In sessions with the mother and aunt, the worker helped them to process their feelings about these difficult issues, as well as their feelings about Lilja having caused her stepbrother's death. They saw it as a terrible accident and did not think Lilja did it intentionally. They expressed regret and anger that the state had taken over, and they could not handle this incident in their own way. The mother and aunt believed that many of Lilja's problems had been the result of being in a mental institution, but they also began to wonder if the family secret might be contributing to her problems.

With the social worker's preparation and support, the mother and aunt decided to tell Lilja the truth about her parentage. Staff were quite concerned about how Lilja might respond to this revelation. However, Lilja revealed that she knew something wasn't right. She thought there was something strange about the way they treated her. Learning the truth was a breakthrough for Lilja; she began to cooperate more with interventions that helped control her behavior. The family came for weekly family therapy sessions. Using a Serbo-Croatian-speaking colleague helped the process, as well as providing valuable insight into Bosnian culture. The stepfather stated that this was the first time anyone in the mental health system had wanted to hear their side of the story.

LEARNING OBJECTIVES

1. Incorporate childhood developmental factors, family dynamics, and sociocultural factors in development of a biopsychosocial assessment.

2. Use the DSM-IV to develop a differential diagnosis for an adult who has serious mental illness.

3. Apply family theory to explain a family's coping mechanisms in light of their culture, family dynamics, family history, and other relevant facts in the case.

4. Develop a culturally relevant multilevel intervention plan. Defend it based on research and theory.

5. Analyze and describe the impact of stigma, discrimination, and oppression on individual and family difficulties.

ACTIVITIES

1. Identify and analyze the biological, psychological, and sociocultural issues that would be taken into account in your assessment of this case. What structural/contextual factors do you see in this case?

2. Using the DSM-IV, discuss how you would develop a diagnosis for Lilja. Referring to the case material, discuss the evidence for the different diagnostic categories you would consider. Based on the case history and diagnostic categories you have selected, explain your prognosis for Lilja.

3. Describe the family dynamics. Discuss the ways in which their coping mechanisms are adaptive and in what ways they are maladaptive. Taking into account the family dynamics and cultural factors, which family theory or theories would be most appropriate in working with this case?

4. Given the "secret" in this family, what are the ethical considerations in protecting confidentiality of family members' communications with you? How would you want to deal with the secret in this case? In small groups, demonstrate using role-play your approach to discussing this with a family member or members.

5. Do you see any issues of stigma, discrimination, and oppression? What interventions would you consider at the individual, family, and community levels.

SUGGESTED READINGS

American Psychiatric Association. (2000). *Diagnostic and statistical manual of mental disorders* (4th ed., Text Rev.). Washington, DC: Author.

Early, T., and GlenMaye, L. (2000). Valuing families: Social work practice with families from a strengths perspective. *Social Work, 45,* 118–130.

Miller, K. E., Worthington, G. J., and Muzurovic, J. (2002). Bosnian refugees and the stressors of exile: A narrative study. *American Journal of Orthopsychiatry, 72,* 341–354.

Nichols, M., and Schwartz, R. (1991). *Family therapy concepts and methods.* Boston: Allyn & Bacon.

5-2 RESETTLEMENT OF A JEWISH REFUGEE FAMILY FROM THE FORMER SOVIET UNION

Introduction

This case study introduces students to the service delivery system for Jewish immigrants to the United States. Students learn about the trauma of moving from one's country of origin and its effects on the physical and emotional state of individuals. In contrast to other refugee groups, Jewish refugees may be offered a comprehensive array of services. The case describes the step-by-step approach used to help families access needed resources and to adjust to their new environment. Students can examine the delivery system in relation to that provided for other ethnic populations in their area.

The case offers an opportunity to learn about a new culture and to apply principles of culturally sensitive practice to a family. Students are directed to critique the continuum of services and to determine what else might be included. Multilevel interventions at the individual, family, programmatic, and community levels are addressed. Relevant theories are ecosystems, family systems, role theory, crisis theory, risk and resilience, and strengths perspective.

Case Study

Jewish Family Service (JFS), under the auspices of Jewish Federation, works with refugees who are qualified to receive assistance. Generally, these refugees are primarily Jewish, from the former Soviet Union and Bosnia, and may include B'hai families from Iran. JFS works closely with the Hebrew Immigration Aid Society (HIAS). In order to emigrate, a prospective immigrant is required to have blood relatives in the United States, such as mother, father, siblings, or children. These relatives usually keep in contact with the local Jewish Family Services.

The Refugee Resettlement Coordinator at JFS provides the relatives with a set of documents that must be completed by the potential immigrants. The completed documents are then mailed to HIAS in New York. After being carefully reviewed, they are submitted to the American Immigration Services in the country of origin. It takes from three to six months for them to assess whether the request for emigration is valid. If assessed positively, the immigrants are assigned a number and then an interview is conducted with the family, usually within the next year or two. The interview is to assess the extent of religious persecution. If the family receives approval as refugees, the information is transmitted to HIAS. It takes an additional year for the family to arrive. HIAS contacts the local JFS Refugee Resettlement Coordinator to gain more information about the initial sponsor for the refugees and to ensure that their plans have not changed. A Sponsorship Agreement is signed defining the responsibilities of each party (JFS and sponsor). The agreement is submitted to HIAS, which then reports to Immigration Services that the case can be accepted.

As soon as the immigrant relatives arrive in the United States, HIAS representatives meet them at the airport—usually a central international hub such as

New York. HIAS support staff assist the new immigrants in applying for federal and private refugee aid. JFS can provide each individual immigrant $500 for the first month of resettlement. Refugees have the right to get food stamps and medical benefits from the local welfare department. Refugees sixty-two years or older and with serious medical conditions can apply for Supplemental Security Income and receive it within one month. The agency assists with housing services and can provide counseling for emotional problems.

The sponsoring relatives are responsible for refugee housing if refugees are unable to pay for their own housing. Generally, sponsoring families provide the initial security deposit for an apartment or a house. Often there are problems in finding affordable housing. Not having a credit history in the United States as well as language barriers can make initial securing of housing difficult. Families may need language assistance and additional financial resources if necessary and appropriate. The agency can provide a loan or refer the family to the Hebrew Free Loan Agency. JFS also assists families in buying food, finding furniture (which is often donated by the Jewish community), and securing telephone service. The agency relies on the assistance of volunteers from the Jewish community.

Relatives are instructed to contact JFS when there are problems such as a missed flight, so that HIAS can be notified. A caseworker will meet with refugees a couple of days after they arrive and provide information about community resources, services, agencies, synagogues, Jewish schools, food stamps, medical services including different hospitals that have translators available, social security, transportation, and English as a Second Language (ESL) schools. Volunteers are involved in providing individual English language tutoring, transportation, and legal immigration assistance (application completion, and classes for naturalization). They also assist with acculturation, inviting families together for Passover, Chanukah, High Holidays (Yom Kippur and Rosh Hashanah), and Shabbat for family sharing. Sometimes JFS will transport refugees to medical appointments and job interviews. Help is also available with job interview skills and creating résumés. Information is provided about the residency requirements for reduced tuition to public colleges. Teachers are informed that they can take the teacher certification test and teach here. A Russian club meets once a month at a local synagogue and includes famous artists, actresses, and opera singers. Assistance and advocacy is provided in dealing with problems related to the Immigration and Naturalization Service. JFS provides a booklet of community resources as well.

Many well-educated refugees bring expectations that do not match real life as an immigrant in the United States. They have to adjust their expectations to reality. Sometimes they become depressed. Quite often they were previously at a high social level in society, working in administrative and influential positions. At home they were "somebody." Coming to the United States they have to accept the fact that their career and social status will start from ground level. For a while, they will be "nobody" here. For example, one man who had a high position in the former Soviet Union came to the United States with very limited English skills. He could not find employment for a long time, not even a low-paying laborer job. He would not let go of his former status and purchased a luxury car the family could not afford. Some people blame others or feel like victims and are frustrated. Men have more difficulty in making the necessary changes in roles and personal identity. They suffer depression because they sometimes feel humiliated by the changes. If a person experiences depression, this impacts his or her whole family. Women often are more realistic and tend to adjust more easily; they hide their pride deep inside and pass their dreams to their children.

Besharov Family

Sara, a JFS caseworker, related the situation of the Besharov family from Kiev, who came to the agency with several concerns. Their car was stolen. The JFS worker assisted them in reporting this to the police. She contacted the insurance company and found multiple resources to secure an automobile if the car was not recovered. People can donate cars for refugees. The family then only pays the cost of registration and vehicle emissions inspection fees. JFS can further help a family by providing a loan. In this case, the family was able to get their muddied, stolen vehicle in good operating condition for the cost of a $160 tow.

This family of four (father, Stepan, fifty-eight; mother, Natasha, fifty-five; son, Boris, thirty-two; daughter, Raisa, seventeen) arrived in June, just as public assistance was cutting back the monthly allotment of food stamps to refugees. It was two months before the family received human assistance and food stamps. In this family, the son, Boris, is largely responsible for bringing income to the whole family unit. Ever since flying to the United States, he has had medical problems such as fainting and nosebleeds. He has been able to secure a job but has passed out at work. Various tests thus far have not produced a diagnosis. The family contacts Sara all the time for moral support and other forms of assistance. The goal for the family is to become self-sufficient, and they depend on Boris for this to happen. An older daughter, Sophia, recently passed away. The son, who is an introvert and keeps everything inside has not expressed his feelings about his sister's death.

Being a Russian Jewish immigrant herself, Sara is able to give assistance based on her experience. She knows how to prioritize problem areas and believes she is a model for successful goal attainment. Also, because she is of the same culture, she believes she can relate to the emotional problems of Russian immigrants. She has a time perspective, and lets people know that the immediate difficulties they face are not forever. She also shares feelings about her own refugee experience.

LEARNING OBJECTIVES

1. Increase your knowledge of needs and concerns of refugees and services available to them.

2. Apply the vulnerable life condition framework, risk and resilience model, crisis intervention, and the strengths perspective to assessment of and interventions for Russian refugees.

3. Increase sensitivity to cultural differences of recent immigrants.

4. Enhance skill in program and service development based on identified unmet need.

ACTIVITIES

1. Using the framework of risk and resilience, identify the factors in the case of the Besharov family and the general information provided about Russian families that contribute to vulnerability.

   a. How has this case enhanced your understanding of the emotions and stresses that a refugee family may experience?
   b. How might they be different from an immigrant family who has been here for several months?
   c. What similarities and differences might there be between this family and a Southeast Asian immigrant family?

2. Discuss your biopsychosocial assessment of this family including an evaluation of their strengths.

3. Jewish Family Services has offered many services to this family to assist them in the immigration adjustment process. Based on your assessment, what other interventions and services might you consider?

4. Assuming you are not of the same culture, how might you go about finding out what cultural factors you need to be aware of in offering help to this family and how to effectively deal with cultural differences? Using role-play, demonstrate how you might speak to the family or a family member about this.

5. Sara, the social worker, identified a number of unmet needs for Russian immigrant families. Among them were (1) the need for low- or no-cost cultural events for different age groups, (2) improved timetable for job searching and job procurement since only a small number are successful in the first month, (3) the need for health benefits during the early months of new employment since many Russian immigrants arrive with previously existing health problems, and (4) support services such as case management and transportation for elderly immigrants.

   Choose one area of unmet need that is of interest to you and discuss the step-by-step intervention strategy that you would follow to address the problem. Are there existing models locally or elsewhere from which you could draw? What obstacles might you encounter?

SUGGESTED READINGS

Balgopal, P. (2000). *Social work practice with immigrants and refugees.* New York: Columbia University Press.

Devore, W., and Schlesinger, E. (1996). Ethnic-sensitive practice with refugees and new immigrants. In *Ethnic-sensitive social work* (4th ed., pp. 241–256). Boston: Allyn & Bacon.

Drachman, D. and Shen Ryan, A. (2001). Immigrants and refugees. In A. Gitterman, *Handbook of social work practice with vulnerable and resilient populations.* New York: Columbia University Press.

Hulewat, P. (1996). Resettlement: A cultural and psychological crisis. *Social Work, 42,* 129–135.

5-3   INTERVENTIONS FOR RECENT HMONG IMMIGRANTS

Introduction

This case study is representative of the experience of many Southeast Asian families when they first come to the United States. In contrast to the previous situation where long-standing services for Jewish immigrants were in place for more recent Soviet refugees, a well-established continuum of services was not available for the Hmong family described in the vignette. Therefore, in addition to family assistance, resource and program development and community organization are key interventions for students to consider. The case is useful for sensitizing students to the need to be aware of differences in subpopulations that may come from the same region and, in particular, presents an opportunity to learn about Hmong culture. Students who do not have the ability to speak the language of this ethnic group must think through the most effective ways of reaching this client population. Applicable theories include family systems, oppression theory, empowerment theory, and the strengths perspective.

Case Study

Ngo Lee, a widowed Hmong woman, arrived in the United States three years ago. She has eight children and lives with her five youngest, ages two to twelve. She was resettled in a small city in the San Joaquin valley of California. The flat terrain is unfamiliar to this woman, who came from a mountain community in Southeast Asia. Ms. Lee is proud of her apartment, and she keeps it well organized. However, due to poor maintenance by the landlord, there is significant molding, faulty electrical wiring, and visibly dilapidating plaster walls.

As there is no heat in the apartment, Ms. Lee has been burning scrap plywood for heat. This wood has likely been treated with chemicals, putting her at risk for unknown side effects. The electric range does not work, most electrical outlets do not work, and an electrical wire is running over the sink to a microwave oven. There is also an exposed electrical outlet on top of the air conditioner.

The immediate neighborhood is a dead-end street with high low-cost rental housing. There are two gangs in constant conflict within the neighborhood as reflected by numerous bullet holes. There used to be numerous crack cocaine dealers in the area, now there are only a few. The graffiti is homogenized into two styles and is prevalent throughout the neighborhood. There are two shops where stolen cars are disguised.

Ms. Lee has received an eviction notice from the city. The conditions of her apartment are clearly below code. Furthermore, because of the gang activity, her children are unsafe when they go outside. There is no stable, affordable residence available to Ms. Lee at this time. However, the welfare office has provided her with money sufficient for three nights at a motel. Ms. Lee is frightened about being forced to leave her apartment complex as there are several Hmong residents and a support network. She does not speak English, and the older children, who might act as translators, have left and their places of residence are unknown. Her youngest children are not learning English as there is no preschool in the nearby vicinity.

In Cambodia, her husband disappeared mysteriously prior to her emigration to the United States. He was likely slain. She lived in the Cambodian forests for three years after the Communists overtook Laos. During this period of time, Ms. Lee was undernourished—her diet consisted primarily of bananas and insects.

In the United States, Ms. Lee's current apartment has been her only home. While by American standards she has not been able to feed her children a normal amount of food, it has been easier here than before. She also has relied significantly on the Hmong community for support. While she has been scared in the United States, her living situation has been an improvement from before.

Ms. Lee is going to experience disruption in her life again, as she will be evicted from her apartment within three days. She will miss the relationships she has established with her Hmong neighbors, but she will continue to receive support from social service agencies serving the Southeast Asian community. She will also continue to receive monthly welfare checks from the county.

You have just obtained your MSW, and your first job is a case manager position at a Southeast Asian resource center. You are expected to perform multiple roles in the community, including outreach, casefinding, information and referral, counseling, community mobilization, and resource development. You speak some Cambodian but are unfamiliar with several Hmong words. Ms. Lee has been assigned to you for assistance. While speaking with Ms. Lee, a neighbor assists you in translation of some specific terms.

LEARNING OBJECTIVES

1. Understand the impact of the social welfare laws on immigrants and learn about the service delivery system available to the Hmong population.

2. Work collaboratively with community-based agencies on behalf of an ethnic population.

3. Provide culturally sensitive interventions to a Hmong family based on knowledge of the Hmong culture.

ACTIVITIES

1. As a social worker, what options would you explore with Ms. Lee in order to respond to her immediate crisis—the eviction notice?

   a. How would you assess and prioritize the options?
   b. What economic and housing assistance would be available to Ms. Lee in your community, and how would you assist her in accessing those services?

2. If you find there are areas of unmet need for people in Ms. Lee's situation, what kind of role might you play, and what strategy would you use in developing needed services in the Hmong community?

3. Assuming you are not Hmong-speaking, discuss the pros and cons of the various ways you might overcome this language barrier in working with Ms. Lee. If you are Hmong-speaking, discuss how this would impact your work with this family.

4. What theoretical perspective(s) would be most effective in working with this family?

SUGGESTED READINGS

Fadiman, A. (1997). *When the spirit catches you, and you fall down.* New York: Farrar, Straus, and Giroux.

Padilla, Y. (1997). Immigrant policy: Issues for social work practice. *Social Work, 42,* 595–606.

HEALTH-RELATED INTERVENTIONS

INTRODUCTION

The cases in this chapter address several issues that social workers in health contexts struggle with frequently. Case 6-1 illustrates a client coping with terminal illness and raises issues about client self-determination in end-of-life decisions, the role of religion in dealing with serious illness, and the impact of social support on a dying client. It provides an opportunity for students to sharpen their knowledge and organizational skills regarding interventions with the interdisciplinary team on behalf of clients, to understand the social work perspective on health care, and to interpret the social work role in the health care setting. Case 6-2 focuses on one of the current challenges in work with persons living with AIDS—assisting with the psychosocial aspects of changing from a terminally ill person to one who, due to current medical advances, can return to normal functioning. In Case 6-3, students study a community that has insufficient health care resources and move from an analysis of the community needs to an analysis of the impact of limited resources on families. Special topics in this chapter include death and dying, AIDS, and developmental disabilities. Latino, African American, and Gay culture can be explored through these cases. Interventions include community organization, community development, program planning and development, and individual and family counseling. Theories covered include the strengths perspective, risk and resilience, organizational theory, role theory, oppression theory, and empowerment theory.

6-1 DEALING WITH ENDSTAGE ILLNESS: CULTURAL ISSUES AND THE INTERDISCIPLINARY TEAM

ROBIN WIGGENS CARTER

Introduction

This case describes a young adult woman who has been diagnosed with terminal breast cancer. She is resisting the treatment recommendations of the health care team and instead relies on her religion and extensive support system for comfort and sustenance. The health care team is concerned about her lack of compliance. Students have an opportunity to consider the social work perspective on health care and how this may be imparted to health care team members who view the situation differently. Students can begin to identify their leadership capabilities in an interdisciplinary environment and explore how they may use those skills on behalf of clients. They learn how to respond to the client's unique coping style in facing terminal illness within the context of client self-determination and making end-of-life decisions. Students struggle with the client's right to self-determination in relation to their responsibility to promote the client's best interests. Risk and resilience, death and dying, social support, oppression, and organizational theories are applicable. Students attend to the role of spirituality in working with clients and apply principles of culturally sensitive practice both with the client system and the health care team.

Case Study

Janelle is a thirty-five-year-old African American single parent of three school-aged children. She was divorced from the father of her twelve-year-old twin sons as well as from the father of her seven-year-old daughter. She is a teacher's aide who has been employed with the same school for more than five years.

Janelle was diagnosed one month ago with metastatic breast cancer. Her medical team wants her to undergo an aggressive round of chemotherapy and possible radiation therapy for palliative treatment. The team believes the treatment will prolong Janelle's life and allow for a higher quality of life in the interim. Janelle is refusing all medical intervention, choosing instead to rely on prayer for healing. Her decision has caused a great deal of tension between Janelle and her medical team. At this point she is refusing all follow-up care.

Janelle reports having some idea that she was ill over a year ago when she felt a lump in her breast while in the shower. She delayed seeking treatment at that time because she had no health insurance benefits and did not have the money to pay for an exam. Later, when her medical benefits were in place, she reports the lump seemed to have gotten smaller—she assumed it was going away, and since she had no further symptoms she did not seek treatment. Janelle's mother finally urged her to see her physician after she saw marked discoloration and what appeared to be a sizable lump on Janelle's breast.

Janelle was at first very cooperative with her medical team. Her oncologist, Dr. Jones, recommended the treatment, and Janelle initially agreed to comply. It was only after Dr. Jones referred Janelle to the hospice program that she began to voice her opposition to further treatment. Janelle had been clear with her physician about her fundamentalist Christian beliefs and in her faith that she would be healed. She sought consultation with her minister, who also encouraged her to comply with the treatment as a supplement to prayer. Her fellow church members organized a prayer chain and a rotating team of members to provide childcare, domestic chores, and ongoing emotional support for Janelle and her children.

The referral to hospice mobilized a team of professionals including a registered nurse, an oncology nurse specialist, an occupational therapist, and a social worker. Since Janelle was not conceding that she was dying, she resented the intrusion of the "professionals," who were more intent on changing her lifestyle than providing support. They determined that Janelle's pleasant, cheerful presentation and her seeming inability to express her fear and sadness about dying was further evidence of her use of denial as a defense. Janelle contends that this was her usual demeanor, and she did not believe she had anything to fear. She believed that she could be healed—and that even if they were right—she had been taught not to fear death. It was Janelle's belief that they were continuously undermining her beliefs, suggesting that she should not rely as much on the advice of others such as her minister and other church members, as they were not medically trained and did not have experience treating people with her medical condition. One of the nurses suggested that Janelle should spend more time on self-care. In addition, Janelle felt judged by the hospice team. She was questioned several times about her decision to delay seeing a physician when she first felt the lump in her breast. They often used terms she did not understand, requiring her to ask repeated questions about her illness. Members of the team seemed uncomfortable in her home, which was small, cluttered, and always filled with people.

Janelle is the oldest of five children. Her father died of prostate cancer two years ago. Janelle shares her home with her fifty-five year old mother, her three children, and two of her youngest sister's children. Four of her siblings live in the area and have been a continual source of emotional and instrumental support for her. As her youngest sister is serving out a prison sentence for a drug-related crime, Janelle and her mother are caring for the children. Janelle's first husband is actively involved with both his children. Her second husband provides no financial support and rarely visits his daughter.

She has been a member of the same church for twenty-five years and is active in many of the church activities. She is a Sunday School teacher and takes pride in the development of a nursery, which she oversees. Janelle refers to the church members as her "second family."

Janelle's perpetual sense of optimism and pleasant, accepting disposition are experienced by everyone who knows her. She has lived in the same community all of her life and seems to know everyone. She is viewed as the community advisor, often taking in neighbors who are experiencing hard times. Her home has always been one of the neighborhood meeting places.

LEARNING OBJECTIVES

1. Analyze and respond to ethical dilemmas in a health care setting.

2. Understand and explain the social work role on the health care interdisciplinary team and develop competence in dealing with interprofessional relationships. Articulate social work values and contribute a social work perspective to the team.

3. Develop leadership skills as a health care team member.

4. Using a strengths perspective, determine and respond to the role of client self-determination in making end-of-life personal/medical decisions.

5. Gain knowledge and skill in responding to client cultural and spiritual/religious issues in the health care context.

ACTIVITIES

1. What ethical dilemmas might you encounter if you were the social worker assigned to work with and on behalf of Janelle. Discuss in your group how you would think through those dilemmas and what decisions you would make.

2. Discuss your reaction to Janelle's decision to delay medical care and to turn to religion to provide healing and comfort for herself. Explain how you reconcile what is in the best interests of the client and client self-determination if they seem to be at odds?

3. Applying a strengths (resilience) perspective, what strengths does Janelle display? How would you include them in your multilevel interventions?

4. What cultural factors do you see as important in this case, and how would you take them into account in your interventions?

5. Taking into account your social work training in organizational and group dynamics and social work values, what strategies might you employ in providing understanding to the team about Janelle so that services to her might be improved?

SUGGESTED READINGS

Abramson, J., and Mizrahi, T. (1996). When social workers and physicians collaborate: Positive and negative interdisciplinary experiences. *Social Work, 41,* 270–281.

Brodsky, A. (1999). "Making it": The components and process of resilience among urban, African-American, single mothers. *American Journal of Orthopsychiatry, 69,* 148–159.

Devore, W., and Schlesinger, E. (1996). Ethnic-sensitive practice in health care. In *Ethnic-sensitive social work practice* (4th ed., pp. 293–322). Boston: Allyn & Bacon.

Holosko, M. J., and Taylor, P. A. (1992). *Social work practice in health care settings* (2nd ed.). Toronto: Canadian Scholars Press.

National Association of Social Workers. (2003). Client self-determination in end-of-life decisions. *Social Work Speaks* (pp. 46–49). Washington, DC: NASW Press.

Rolland, J. (1993). Mastering family challenges in serious illness and disability. In F. Walsh, (Ed.), *Normal family processes* (pp. 444–473). New York: Guilford.

Walsh, F. (1999). *Spiritual resources in family therapy.* New York: Guilford.

6-2 AIDS IN REMISSION: REVERSING DIRECTION

Introduction

The advent of combination drug therapies in the late 1990s presented new challenges to persons living with AIDS and their providers. A cohort of persons who had exhausted their treatment options and were diagnosed as terminally ill suddenly found themselves revived and facing new challenges for living. The ensuing case study presents many of the issues and one type of scenario that providers encountered. In this situation, the client has been receiving hospice services and has come to grips with his impending death. The reversal of his condition comes as a shock and presents significant existential dilemmas. Students confront the psychodynamic factors in changing one's role as a dying person to a person who has an extended life. The client in this case is unable to make the change. The case demonstrates the lag in shifting service delivery to meet rapid changes and raises issues about how the system could have been more ready for this client. Ecosystems theory, systems theory, role theory, psychodynamic theory, and theories of death and dying are applicable. Multilevel interventions include program development, organizational change, and individual counseling.

Case Study

Dave is a thirty-one-year-old gay Caucasian male diagnosed with AIDS, Hepatitis A, B, and C, and Cirrhosis of the liver. He entered a hospice when he was advised that he was not expected to live more than six months. He moved out of his apartment and gave away all of his belongings to friends and family members.

When Dave first came to the hospice, he isolated himself from the rest of the residents. He did not identify with them, denied his terminal status, and stated that he would stay a few months until he got better and then he would leave. He was angry that he had AIDS when so many others whose lifestyle was similar to his did not. Dave was angry at his family, friends, hospice residents, and staff. He began to think about fathering a child and reasoned that he just wanted to live long enough to have a baby and see him or her before he died. Once he faced his terminal status, he became quite depressed while at the hospice and took antidepressants to alleviate some of the anguish. He started the mourning process, not only for his life, but also for the loss of body functions, ability and energy to hang out with friends, the strength to work, unspoken words, and failed relationships. Dave knew he had AIDS, there was no cure, and he was not going to get better. Eventually, he helped the other residents through their own emotional struggles and was at peace with himself and his family.

It became apparent within the next several months that he was improving, in part due to new combination medications and also due to improved nutrition and sleep. His T cells went up, his viral load went down, he gained weight, and had a resurgence of energy. After he lived in the hospice for over a year, he was asked to leave because he no longer was considered terminally ill.

Dave had given away the contents of his apartment and had spent the entire lump sum retirement allotment his employer had sent him. He felt as if he had nowhere to go, and only $650 on which to live. His family, who lived out of state, had never been supportive throughout his illness and was of no help to him now. His housing was unstable as he moved among his few friends. After moving out of the hospice, he became overwhelmed with his situation and the possibility of a future. He had not planned for a new stage after accepting his impending death. Dave became depressed and began to abuse his medications, alienating friends and medical providers. He also began drinking, thus exacerbating his already compromised liver condition, and consequently retained significant amounts of fluids, which led to his death shortly thereafter. It appeared that he had continued his original plan to die and embarked on a self-destructive course.

Dave was one of the first AIDS patients to receive tri-drug therapy in 1996. During his stay at the hospice, he received care and social work services. Upon his release from the hospice, he continued to receive outpatient medical care, but there were not yet social services in place specifically for persons in his situation living with AIDS, since no one had anticipated the results of the new drug therapy.

LEARNING OBJECTIVES

1. Comprehend the psychosocial issues faced by persons whose health dramatically improves after facing near death due to serious illness.

2. Apply assessment and intervention skills to AIDS as a specific life condition.

3. Enhance knowledge of the service delivery system for persons living with AIDS. Determine adequacy of services, identify unmet needs, and recommend solutions.

ACTIVITIES

1. Develop a concise, well-articulated, biopsychosocial assessment for Dave. Include sexual orientation, developmental stage, and theory about death and dying in your consideration. Choose a partner and take turns presenting your assessment.

2. Assume you are the hospice social worker responsible for discharging Dave back into the community. Based on the case, describe the multilevel intervention plan you would develop in order to provide optimum services for Dave. Discuss with other students in your group how you would prioritize your efforts and explain your step-by-step approach. Consider individual, family, group, and community interventions.

3. Explain the various risks related to Dave's medical conditions—AIDS, Cirrhosis, and Hepatitis.

4. What kinds of services are available to people with AIDS receiving combination drug therapies in the community in which you have your field placement? Analyze their adequacy and make recommendations if appropriate.

SUGGESTED READINGS

Parkes, C. M. (1993). Bereavement as a psychosocial transition: Processes of adaptation to change. In M. Stroebe and W. Strobe (Eds.), *Handbook of bereavement* (pp. 91–101). Cambridge, MA: Cambridge University Press.

Poindexter, C. C. (1997). In the afermath: Serial crisis intervention for people with HIV. *Health and Social Work, 22,* 125–132.

Shernoff, M. (Ed.). (1999). *AIDS and mental health practice.* Binghamton, NY: Haworth Press.

Worden, W. (1991). *Grief counseling and grief therapy: A handbook for the mental health practitioner.* Springfield, IL: Springer.

6-3 NORTHEAST VALLEY: A LATINO COMMUNITY OVERCOMING VULNERABILITY

CANDELARIA PEREZ-DAVIDSON

Introduction

This case study provides an opportunity for students to study the relationship between social factors and family health and to develop multilevel interventions to address both systems. A Latino community in a large city has limited access to general health services, apparently related to ethnic and economic discrimination. Other more affluent and powerful communities are served. The case situation directs students to move from population- and community-focused assessment to individual and family concerns. The specific example involves services to families with children who have developmental delays. Families become aware that they are not alone and begin to seek remedies that will benefit their community. Students consider culturally relevant interventions including community prevention, resource development, individual and family treatment, and rehabilitation through the life cycle of the person with the developmental disability. Applicable theoretical frameworks are empowerment theory, grief and loss, social stratification, community asset mapping, and public health models. The ethical responsibility of social workers to promote social justice is also addressed.

Case Study

The Northeast Valley is a community located within the larger Valley City metropolitan area. The community is predominantly Mexican and Mexican American, low income, and comprises many who work in jobs without health insurance or other benefits. There is also a sizable population of non-English-speaking and undocumented families. It is an area with limited access to health care and has been designated by the State Department of Health Planning and Development as a medically underserved area.

A concern about the community's health problems by community activists has led to the formation of a grassroots organization known as the Northeast Valley Health Task Force (Task Force) of Dorado County, which is committed to improving health care access for its residents. This group, composed of community residents, activists, and social agency representatives, has identified increasing residents' access to health care, including access to preventive health services delivered by culturally competent practitioners, as goals.

The Task Force developed in response to a high rate of preventable health problems in the Northeast Valley, limited access to health providers in the community, and the limited input the Northeast Valley has had in the health planning process in Dorado County and at the state level. The Task Force thinks that the community has pressing health needs that are being ignored. Northeast Valley has the least number of public health clinics of any section of its size in the county. County health officials have placed few clinics in the area, indicating that the people prefer to use *curanderos* and other cultural folk cures. At the state level within the State Department of Health, the Northeast Valley has found the placement of health facilities to be a highly political process in which those communities able to muster the most political influence often have health facilities placed in their community.

The first success of the Task Force was convincing the County Health Department and local Regional Center for the Developmentally Disabled to develop early intervention services for children at the County Health Center by adding a developmental disabilities diagnostic clinic. The Task Force advocated for the clinic in response to Northeast Valley parents' request that they be able to receive medical and social services within the community for their children with suspected developmental delays. This DD Clinic staff comprises a social worker, nurse, and physician. The staff diagnose and case manage infants through children six years of age who are developmentally delayed and provide support services to the children's parents. The clinic is held one half day a month at the Northeast Valley Health Center, and, until recently, part-time employees staffed the entire clinic and none were actually housed at Northeast Valley. The first full-time staff member hired and located at Northeast Valley is a social worker. The addition of a full-time social worker to the clinic is a result of the growth in the clinic's caseload.

As the clinic's recently hired social worker, you are learning about the problems the Northeast Valley parents with developmentally disabled children face in obtaining care for their children. There are few services for the developmentally disabled located in Northeast Valley. When children are referred to services such as physical therapy, dental services, or special preschool education programs, parents must travel across town to obtain care. Many parents do not own cars and find that public transportation presents a major hardship. Often families are referred to service providers who do not have staff that speak Spanish or understand the culture.

While you have been able to develop a list of resources with Spanish-speaking staff and tapped into transportation resources for families, Mrs. Ortiz's visit to your office starts you thinking about the needs of the children that you are currently serving as they grow into adolescence and the connection between lack of health care and children's developmental disabilities. Mrs. Ortiz is a fifty-three-year-old woman with two developmentally disabled sons, a twenty-eight-year-old and an eight-year-old. She has come to see you because she believes that you are an expert who can help her and other parents she knows who have developmentally disabled adult children. These parents are at a loss as to how to care for their children who have outgrown the special education programs in the public schools. Their children are at home with few social contacts and often become depressed and decompensate. Many of the parents are in their late sixties and seventies and are concerned about how their children will be cared for when the parents can no longer care for them. These parents would like their developmentally disabled children to participate in sheltered workshop programs where they can learn life and job skills and socialize with other adults. The parents would also like help in making arrangements for their children's future care.

The reason Mrs. Ortiz initially gives for coming to see you is that she wants you to work with her and the parents to find resources for their children. She would also like help in finding a way to prevent the problems that she has had in her family due to lack of health care and lack of knowledge. Mrs. Ortiz begins telling her story, she says, so that you will understand some of the problems that families in the community have experienced.

Mrs. Ortiz did not receive prenatal care until late in her pregnancy because her husband's employer did not provide health insurance, and she was unaware of community resources. After the birth of her first son, who was developmentally disabled, Mrs. Ortiz gave birth to two healthy daughters. At the age of forty-five when she became pregnant again, she and her husband were pleased because he wanted a "health" son. After some tests during her first trimester of pregnancy, Mrs. Ortiz was told that the fetus had a chromosomal anomaly known as Down Syndrome. She was given the option of an abortion. Although Mrs. Ortiz considered herself marginally Catholic—for example, she had used birth control to space her children—she could not bring herself to have an abortion and decided to carry her son to term. She mentions that she has found the meeting with other parents with developmentally disabled children very supportive but has not been able to involve her husband. Mrs. Ortiz says that for many years he was very angry about the boy's problems, but now she says that he just seems to be sad.

When Mrs. Ortiz finishes talking about her family's history, she states that she knows that you work with families that have younger children, but she wishes you could help her because she has nowhere else to turn. She shares with you the problems she is facing in obtaining medical and dental care for her youngest son, her fear for her sons' future when she and her husband are gone, and her wish to be able to talk with her husband about his sadness.

LEARNING OBJECTIVES

1. Analyze a complex community situation and be able to link the impact of community problems with family/individual problems.

2. Describe and analyze the social work role in remedying the consequences of social problems.

3. Discuss the obligations of social workers to work to address the causes of the underlying problems, based on the relevant sections of the NASW Code of Ethics.

4. Identify and defend appropriate culturally sensitive multilevel strategies that social workers can use to intervene.

5. Select and apply the theoretical frameworks of empowerment, grief and loss, community asset mapping, and social stratification.

ACTIVITIES

1. Describe and analyze the community, program/service delivery, and individual/family level issues in this case. How would you prioritize them? Defend your rationale for their priority. What connection, if any, do you see between community conditions and Mrs. Ortiz's concerns?

2. In what ways is the ethnic profile of the community related to your definition of the problem, and how does it affect potential solutions?

3. Describe the multilevel interventions that you would use at the community, family, and individual levels. What theoretical frameworks would you use to explain the dynamics at each level? Which theoretical frameworks provide bridges or connections between the levels?

4. What sections of the NASW Code of Ethics provide guidance to you regarding your obligations to seek remedies for the underlying social justice problems in this case?

SUGGESTED READINGS

Davis, B. H. (1987). Disability and grief. *Social Casework, 68,* 352–357.

Kretzmann, J., and McKnight, J. (1993). *Building communities from the inside out: A path toward finding and mobilizing a community's assets.* Evanston, IL: Center for Urban Affairs and Policy Research, Northwestern University.

Naperstek, A., and Dooley, D. (1997). Countering urban disinvestment through community building initiatives. *Social Work, 42,* 506–514.

NASW Code of Ethics. (1999). Washington, DC: NASW Press.

Page-Adams, D., and Sherraden, M. (1997). Asset building as a community revitalization strategy. *Social Work, 42,* 409–536.

Seligman, M. (1991). *The family with a handicapped child.* Boston: Allyn & Bacon.

CHAPTER SEVEN

MULTILEVEL INTERVENTIONS WITH ORGANIZATIONS AND COMMUNITIES

INTRODUCTION

The cases in this chapter cover program planning, integrative practice, and social work interventions in the administrative role. Special topics include prevention, services to American Indians, spirituality, supervision, administration, and program evaluation. Case 7-1 provides a detailed example of the planning process in development of a parenting program. Since most students have little exposure to prevention practice, this case allows students to follow a step-by-step approach to a population-focused intervention rather than to develop their own as in other cases in this volume. Student problem solving occurs by applying the principles learned in another problem. The case illustrates community needs assessment, community mobilization, client involvement in planning, culturally competent practice, and task-oriented group work.

Case 7-2 focuses on the role of a social worker in a multiservice agency that requires the ability to work with the community, supervise staff, and provide direct services to clients. The case demonstrates how the social worker moves back and forth between and among these roles. Students learn the importance of cultural sensitivity in community interventions, staff relationships, and client contacts. The case provides an opportunity to study all levels of practice within the context of the American Indian culture.

Case 7-3 presents the relationships among clinical services, program development, and research. The setting is a multiservice center for older adults that has implemented an innovative program at four service sites to enhance the physical and emotional health of patients by placing social workers in outpatient primary care practices. Research is a significant part of the program design. Students can study the differences in program implementation among the four sites, interdisciplinary issues in the health setting, and the role of the social worker in providing health services to the elderly.

Case 7-4 presents a typical example of administrative challenges faced by social workers. The organization described has moved through various stages and is undergoing significant change. Students must accurately assess the organizational situation and determine the most appropriate interventions in order to help the agency regain equilibrium. Professional leadership styles and strategies can be studied in this context.

7-1 PRIMARY PREVENTION TO PROMOTE EFFECTIVE PARENTING: THE PARENT UNIVERSITY

PATRICIA C. WYRICK

Introduction

This case study provides a step-by-step description of a community planning process for a primary prevention program to promote effective parenting skills. Since many students have not had experience with either prevention or planning, the inclusion of planning details gives students tools that are transferable to other areas that may interest them. The model presented demonstrates how to engage the beneficiaries of the program in planning, involve key community organizations, and pay heed to cultural diversity in planning educational and social events. In this case, the planners are sensitive to the needs of the large Spanish-speaking population in the community as well as to the presence of gay and lesbian families. The case utilizes needs assessment to inform the project. Students are asked to design an evaluation instrument. Students consider the role of social work in primary prevention. They apply the planning principles described in the case to another issue of interest to reinforce learning. Key interventions are community organization, planning, and program evaluation. Relevant frameworks are the public health model, empowerment theory, and family systems theory.

Case Study

Parent University Planning Overview

About the Parent University The Parent University is a project that was undertaken by the Verbena County Family Resource Network in collaboration with many other agencies serving families and children in Verbena County. The Parent University consists of a one-day event that offers parents an opportunity to access parent education classes, workshops, networking opportunities, parenting information, and other resources to assist them in raising and nurturing their children.

This event, entitled "Growing Healthy Children in the 21st Century" was held at Verbena Community College.

Target Population In selecting the target population, the main factors considered were need and service gaps. Because recent Parent Universities had targeted parents of teenagers and children with special needs, the planning committee decided to focus on parents of children from birth to age twelve. The project hoped to reach a minimum of two hundred parents.

Project Goals The primary goal of the project is to improve the quality of life of families and children by promoting parental capacity to provide a safe and nurturing environment where children can grow and thrive. An additional goal is to make the content as meaningful as possible for parents and to ensure that it meets their needs.

Some of the strategies to accomplish these goals include:

- Parent/consumer involvement
- Parent/consumer input
- Addressing potential access barriers such as child care, transportation, and language
- Addressing diversity issues
- Providing incentives for parents to attend, including a resource fair
- Comprehensive outreach efforts
- Providing both lectures and "how-to" workshops
- Providing follow-through
- Conducting evaluation to obtain feedback for improvement of future events

Organizational Structure The initial organizers of the Parent University were the Verbena Family Resource Center Network in partnership with Regional Health Maintenance Organization. Other agencies serving families and children were invited to participate in the Planning Committee. Some of the collaborating organizations included County Office of Education, Verbena Community College, Head Start, and Healthy Start programs. Funding needed to implement the project was provided by some of the collaborative partners. Additional funds were raised from vendors attending the Resource Fair.

The planning group was divided into a steering committee and several subcommittees in order to do the detailed work. Each subcommittee had a coordinator representing each group at the steering committee. Nine subcommittees were established:

- Five workshop subcommittees to plan for the workshops in each of the five content areas selected by parents
- Special needs subcommittee to address transportation and other special needs
- Child care subcommittee

- Facilities/Vendors subcommittee
- Diversity subcommittee

Content and Format The workshop content was based on the results of the parent survey. Five definite themes stood out in the survey results: Bringing out the best in your child, communicating with your children, taking care of yourself, neighborhood safety, and teen parenting. Family reading and math were also top items. These topics were seen as too specific; therefore, the committee decided to fold them under "Bringing out the best in your child." The five top priorities identified were the same for English- and Spanish-speaking parents. The format consisted of five strands, one for each of the themes selected. Each strand offered at least a morning session and an afternoon session, covering topics within the specific theme. Seven workshops were offered in each session to accommodate the two hundred parents attending. The following format was selected to structure the event for the subcommittee's planning.

Strategies Utilized to Achieve Goals (Interventions)

Parent/Consumer Involvement Parent volunteers were given a stipend of $200 distributed in three payments (beginning of planning, midway, and end). A total of twelve parent/consumer volunteers participated.

Parent/Consumer Input-In order to gather as much input as possible from parents regarding the content of the classes or workshops, the planning committee chose to conduct a survey of parents. The survey instrument was prepared both in English and Spanish and was distributed to parents at the Family Resource Center and at elementary school sites. Additionally, the committee conducted two focus groups with children aged ten to twelve to determine their view on what their parents need to know to communicate better with them or to have a better relationship with them.

Addressing Access Barriers In order to make the event accessible to working parents, the event was scheduled on a Saturday. To get a sense of the extent and types of barriers that may prevent parents from attending, questions regarding transportation, translation, and child care needs were included in the survey. The main need identified by parents was child care (forty respondents), five parents checked transportation, and twelve parents checked English/Spanish translations.

Addressing Diversity Issues Some of the steps to ensure that diversity was addressed included the following:

1. Inviting parents/consumers representing the county's diversity. There were three Hispanic volunteers, one Filipino–Native American, and one Mien parent. One of the participants was a grandparent raising grandchildren.

2. Being as inclusive as possible in addressing diversity, including race, ethnicity, culture, and sexual orientation.
3. Enlisting help of experts on cultural competence issues.
4. Using members within each diverse group to conduct outreach.
5. Planning workshops that are relevant to the diverse populations in the county.
6. Considering curriculums and models available that have proven to be effective, such as "Young Men as Fathers," "Effective Black Parenting Program," "Los Niños Bien Educados," and so forth.
7. Using bilingual presenters, rather than translators, whenever possible.
8. Providing a variety of foods that may appeal to people from different cultures. To accomplish this, different ethnic organizations assisted in providing food.

Providing Incentives for Parents to Attend There were door prizes and a raffle at the end of the event. Raffles were obtained through vendors, businesses, and private donors. There were also prizes for the children. Food and refreshments, including breakfast and lunch for adults and children, were provided. A resource fair provided information on community resources for families.

Comprehensive Outreach Efforts
How. Getting flyers and registration forms out early, outreach to clients served by collaborative partners, distributing flyers to other organizations, media and meeting announcements, enlisting the help of parent/grandparents participating in the planning.

Who. Faith community, word of mouth, kinship groups, day care providers and child development centers, Verbena Community College students, teen parents, parents court-ordered to attend, diverse ethnic groups, and gay, lesbian, bisexual, and transgender groups.

Providing Both Lectures and "How-to" Workshops The content of the workshops included both traditional presentations and "how-to" workshops for parents who wanted to engage in community organizing and advocacy efforts beyond the one-day event. Proposed activities included childcare co-ops, neighborhood safety, community capacity building, informal networks, and advocacy. Follow-through was provided to ensure success of organizing efforts.

Providing Follow-Through The committee ensured that parents who were interested in community organizing or networking initiatives could get assistance in doing so. Follow-up ideas included planning ahead of time for post-event activities and providing parents with a specific contact person to follow up with for each post-event activity.

Evaluation to Obtain Feedback for Improvement of Future Events An evaluation survey was designed and distributed to participants to obtain feedback that could be used to enhance or improve future events.

LEARNING OBJECTIVES

1. Describe and interpret the role of the social worker in designing effective social and emotional health promotion programs.

2. Learn about resources that are population- and prevention-focused.

3. Design a prevention program in an area of interest that indicates your ability to apply the principles extracted from the Parent University model.

4. Develop a program evaluation instrument that includes process and outcome measures.

ACTIVITIES

1. Discuss the role of social work in prevention. Identify prevention programs in the community surrounding your field placement. Using these examples, readings, and your field experience, describe the functions that social workers use in prevention at multiple levels (individual, family, group, organizational, and community).

2. After reviewing the proposed plan in this vignette, what guiding principles do you think were used in developing the Parent University?

3. Identify an area of interest that would lend itself to a preventive approach. Which principles from the case vignette would apply and which would not? Based on your area of interest, design a prevention program drawing on the Parent University model and adding elements of your own to fit your area.

4. How would you design a multifaceted evaluation for the Parent University. What indicators would you use in order determine whether the program was successful? Include both programmatic indicators and effective parenting indicators. What measurement tools would you use for each?

SUGGESTED READINGS

Bond, L., and Burns, C. (1998). Investing in parents' development as an investment in primary prevention. *Journal of Mental Health,* 7, 493–504.

Fraser, M., Randolph, K., and Bennett, M. D. (2000). Prevention: A risk and resilience perspective. In C. Garvin and P. Allen-Meares (Eds.), *The handbook of social work direct practice* (pp. 89–111). Thousand Oaks, CA: Sage.

Royse, D. (1996). *Program evaluation: An introduction.* Belmont, CA: Thomson Learning-Wadsworth.

7-2 INTEGRATED SERVICES IN AMERICAN INDIAN COUNTRY

WYNNE DuBRAY

Introduction

In many comprehensive multiservice programs, social workers are called on to engage in multiple levels of practice at an advanced level. The multiple roles in this case include community organizer, administrator, supervisor, clinician, and resource developer. The case provides an example of the versatile practitioner who is able to integrate all levels of practice into her work. The hallmark of an advanced practitioner is the ability to move skillfully from one practice level to another as needed. The social worker must be able to deal with staff, clients, community members, and other organizations essential to the well-being of the constituency served by her agency. Students are introduced to cultural issues among American Indians and learn to apply culturally sensitive interventions at all levels. To enhance learning, students can compare strategies for this cultural group with other groups that they work with. Empowerment theory, oppression theory, and community development frameworks are applicable. Students consider the continuum of mental health services from prevention to treatment. Issues of spirituality are also addressed.

Case Study

Mary Sweetgrass, MSW, has accepted a position in Northern California as Director of Behavioral Health for a federally funded comprehensive health clinic providing medical, mental health, substance abuse treatment, health education, dental, and outreach services to several tribes indigenous to the area. Her duties are to provide comprehensive behavioral health services to a caseload of ten clients and supervise a staff of six counselors and one secretary.

Advanced Generalist Perspective

The counselors in this Behavioral Health Unit function as outreach workers, going into homes of clients and conducting family counseling sessions when needed. They visit jails, hospitals, court hearings, and public schools and provide a variety of services. The Behavioral Health Unit offers weight-loss workshops, stress management services, HIV education workshops, parenting workshops, clinical mental health services, community dinners, child welfare services, court advocacy, summer youth programs, after-school youth programs, field trips, play therapy, couples counseling, and workshops for American Indian Elders. They intervene at multiple levels on a regular basis in order to provide comprehensive services to American Indian clients of all ages. The staff is expected to attend tribal community functions as a means of showing their interest and investment in the community.

Coordination

Mary's first tasks are to evaluate the services of her unit, update the policies, procedures, and protocols for specific services, meet with the staff of her unit, and examine clinical records. In addition, she will set up weekly in-service training sessions, weekly case conferences, and weekly staff meetings. She is introducing new intake sheets and statistical record sheets in order to measure the productivity of her staff in carrying out the scope of work identified in federal, state, and nonprofit agency contracts. She is also becoming familiar with her staff by meeting for a minimum of one hour weekly with each staff member for supervision.

Since Mary is a licensed clinical social worker, she will provide direct services to ten clients and/or couples/families. She will also meet with the physicians on staff and discuss with them plans of coordination between her unit and the medical unit. She will meet with the medical staff weekly to discuss referrals and provide feedback for coordination of mental health services with the medical services. She will meet with the Health Educator and coordinate nutrition services and HIV workshops for the hundreds of clients being served by the staff in her unit.

Staff Meeting

At the first staff meeting, Mary's staff shared with her several problems in the community to which the unit needs to respond. First of all, the local school district has been suspending a number of American Indian children at elementary, middle school, and high school levels at higher than normal rates. In addition, many of these teenagers are entering the criminal justice system and are being held at juvenile hall for a number of minor charges. A large proportion are being sent to the California Youth Authority for petty theft charges. The staff does not have access to the Juvenile Detention Center except to visit during visiting hours. A number of adults are being held in the local jails for arrests associated with alcoholism and drug abuse. The staff do not have access to visiting these clients except during family visiting hours. A number of incarcerated minors have been given psychological tests, which have been problematic in that they have scored high on antisocial behavior and have been given longer sentences in the courts. Traditional health practices of a tribal nature were also discussed, as many clients were not satisfied with being treated with Western medicine only.

Action Plan

Mary and her staff developed the following plan to resolve and alleviate some of these issues:

1. Set up a community meeting with American Indian parents as a group to discuss and collect data on suspensions.

2. Meet with the Probation Department to discuss adult and juvenile cases and plan advocacy strategies.

3. Meet with the Director of the County Jail to arrange better access for staff in visiting clients.

4. Meet with the Superintendent of Schools and American Indian Parents to investigate school policies regarding suspensions.

5. Meet with the County Mental Health staff to discuss comprehensive inpatient services to incarcerated American Indian juveniles and adults.

6. Arrange for a professional photographer to visit the Behavioral Health Unit to create photo identification badges for all counselors.

7. Meet with the local traditional healers to assist clients in their utilization of traditional healers when requested.

Progress

1. The meetings resulted in the American Indian Parents attending school board meetings and placing on the agenda the problem of discriminatory suspensions for American Indian children. At the first board meeting, the board tended to ignore the parent group. After the second board meeting was attended by invited reporters from the local newspaper, the board became more interested in the problem. This problem was eventually worked out in a manner that treated the American Indian children fairly.

2. The meeting with probation and jail personnel resulted in greater access for the Behavioral Health staff to juvenile hall and the county jail. In addition, psychological assessments would be referred to the Behavioral Health Unit, which had much greater expertise in understanding the American Indian culture. Juveniles would be referred to the unit, and staff would assume the role of adjunct probation supervisors. This meeting also resulted in American Indian clients being given the choice of going into substance abuse treatment facilities rather than serving time in the county jail.

3. The meeting with County Mental Health resulted in more effective services to incarcerated American Indians who were in need of psychotropic and/or antidepressant medications. A Behavioral Health staff representative was invited to meet with the Mental Health staff at their regular weekly staff meetings for better follow-up of hospitalized American Indian clients. One incarcerated client was also provided advocacy, which resulted in a new trial and release from the County Jail.

4. The director of the Behavioral Health Unit met with the local traditional healers and worked out a plan to provide transportation, lodging, and meals to clients requesting traditional healing ceremonies for mental and physical/spiritual problems.

LEARNING OBJECTIVES

1. Demonstrate knowledge and skill in developing services and programs for an American Indian tribe using multilevel interventions.

2. Demonstrate your ability to develop culturally sensitive preventive interventions.

3. Describe differences and similarities in cultures and apply that knowledge differentially.

4. Increase skill in administration and management of a small service unit that is part of a comprehensive health program.

ACTIVITIES

1. Describe the continuum of interventions that you see in this case from individual/family to organization/community. In what ways is Mary Sweetgrass addressing prevention issues, in what ways solutions to existing problems?

2. How are American Indian cultural issues addressed in this case? Are there any ways they are not being addressed? Discuss this case in light of oppression and empowerment theory.

3. Assuming you are of a different culture, how would you develop a multilevel intervention plan that is culturally sensitive to address staff and community concerns? What would be your goals and objectives? How would you prioritize the steps you would take? Draw a chart showing needs/problems, goals for each, and the evaluation measurement you would use to determine your success in reaching your goals.

4. Discuss how you might approach cultural issues differently or similarly if the community you were serving were Mexican farm workers living in an employer-sponsored migrant camp.

SUGGESTED READINGS

DuBray, W. (1998). *Human services and American Indians* (2nd ed.). Cincinnati, OH: BrooksCole/Thomson Learning.

DuBray, W. (2000). *Mental health interventions with people of color* (2nd ed.). Cincinnati, OH: Thomson Learning.

Gutierrez, L., GlenMaye, L., and DeLois, K. (1995). The organizational context of empowerment practice: Implications for social work administration. *Social Work, 40,* 249–258.

Weaver, H. (1999). Indigenous people in a multicultural society. *Social Work, 43,* 197–202.

7-3 PARTNERS IN CARE: ENHANCING MEDICAL AND PSYCHOSOCIAL CARE FOR THE ELDERLY

Introduction

This case study demonstrates the relationship among clinical services, program development, and research in a large multiservice agency for the elderly. It describes the implementation of an innovative pilot program to provide social work services to older adults in outpatient primary care medical practices. The new program aims to replicate a program for the elderly that was developed in another part of the country and adds a strong research evaluation component. The program intervention focuses on assessment of depression and cognitive impairment and social work interventions. Students become more aware of the needs and concerns of adults over sixty-five years of age and their professional caregivers. They gain understanding of the multiple roles undertaken by a social worker who is a clinical director as well as those of frontline social workers responsible for implementing a new program. They struggle with interdisciplinary relationships and analyze organizational differences among service sites and their impact on program implementation. Students develop intervention strategies based on the different client populations at each site as well as the different organizational cultures. Multilevel interventions include assessment of the elderly, information and referral, care management, program development, program implementation, organizational change, interdisciplinary team management, needs assessment, staff development, and program evaluation. Relevant theoretical frameworks are systems theory, organizational theory, role theory, and developmental theory.

Case Study

The Center for Jewish Older Adults (CJOA) is a service and advocacy agency in a large urban area in the Midwest. It began as a small, community-based storefront operation providing referral and advocacy assistance to the elderly and their families twenty-five years ago. The organization has expanded during that period, has a multimillion dollar budget, and occupies space in a large, modern building, which houses a number of services for the Jewish community. CJOA has a highly developed system of multiple levels of housing for the elderly, ranging from independent living to skilled nursing care. The agency provides a variety of social services, including support for caregivers, transportation, cultural events, lectures, support groups, counseling, and information and referral.

Two years ago, the clinical director, Rose Greenfeld, an LCSW, determined that the agency could accommodate additional services for the elderly community. Based on information from families and service providers, it was evident that ambulatory elderly who were living in their own homes were not gaining access to the array of services that would maintain an optimal quality of life. Many older persons were regularly in contact with their primary care physician but were not being evaluated for their psychosocial needs nor were they requesting services.

The director, who was active nationally in professional associations on behalf of the elderly, became aware of a pilot program based in the West, located in the offices of primary care physicians, which was designed to enhance primary care for older adults through improved access to social services. The program found that using social workers could enhance the outcomes of medical care as well as assess for common problems such as depression and cognitive loss. She brought this information to the medical director of the research department, who would serve as the principal investigator. The agency decided to conduct a replication study that could further develop its collaboration with the medical community as well as enhance its client base.

Rose, whose responsibilities included administration, provision of clinical services, clinical supervision, staff development, program development, and research, was instrumental in leading a collaborative effort among the clinical, development, and research departments of the agency to write a grant proposal as a demonstration project to show the replicability of the program. A small HMO-based primary care group practice was chosen as the first site based on the CJOA's previously held relationships with the physicians and their receptivity to the idea of having a social worker. Funding, which was secured from a small foundation, enabled a CJOA social worker to receive referrals and conduct case finding one day a week. The first site was in a suburban area in close proximity to the city and served an upper-middle to high-income, primarily white population. The research department began to develop profiles of the patients in order to determine the extent of need.

Over the next year, three more sites were started with several different funding sources. A project director was hired to administer the program, coordinate the sites, and oversee the research component. Sites two and three received funds from a large Jewish philanthropic trust that had a specific interest in serving lower-income communities. It recommended a link with one of the Jewish hospitals in the city that had outpatient clinics in several different areas. The project decided on two locations, one near the hospital that served the African American and Hispanic communities, and one on the north side of the city, which primarily served recent Russian immigrants. The hospital wanted jurisdiction over the project social workers in the clinics and negotiated with CJOA to do the hiring. A fourth site was set up shortly thereafter at a private medical practice with whom the clinical director had a relationship, in one of the more affluent areas of the city.

All sites started out with six months of baseline patient data collected by researchers affiliated with the project to determine characteristics of the population and need for services. All had the same focus of assessing for cognitive impairment and depression. Each site developed differently and presented different challenges. In site one there was good rapport between the physicians and the social worker; however, the patients didn't seem to have the need for services that were anticipated. When they did need services, referrals were often dictated by the HMOs. In the sites affiliated with the hospital, start-up was delayed because of hiring problems due to difficulty in finding a Russian-speaking social worker and the low salary budgeted in the grant application. At the onset, considerable time was spent in establishing working relationships with the interdisciplinary team and in interpreting the role of the social worker to ensure that appropriate referrals would be made. A good relationship was established between the social worker and the physicians in the private practice setting; however, the site had difficulties in accepting the research component. Also, the roles of the nurse practitioner and the new social worker needed to be clarified.

The social workers met regularly as a group with the clinical director and the project director to share experiences and to make adjustments in the program as it unfolded. They determined that only patients age sixty-five and older were to be included in the study. It was expected that it would take eighteen to twenty-two months to recruit patients into the study cohort. The group agreed that the social work intervention needed to be developed further and be more clearly defined. The goal was to demonstrate the social work role as a primary care provider in the medical care setting. The social worker would be instrumental in creating a more holistic approach to health care for the elderly. The physicians who already had experience with the elderly would gain knowledge about the psychosocial aspects of their patients' health. The doctors, who were happy to collaborate with the social workers, were not always clear on what were appropriate tasks for them. Therefore, much discussion centered around how to demonstrate the types of services provided by social workers and how to help physicians understand the appropriate role of social workers.

Finally, the directors, social workers, and research staff talked about improving the measures that would be indicators of the project outcomes. How could they show that the presence of social workers improves the health of older adults, improves the knowledge of physicians about the elderly, improves physician knowledge about the social work role, and helps reduce medical costs by providing psychosocial care?

LEARNING OBJECTIVES

1. Enhance ability to integrate program development and implementation, clinical intervention, and research.

2. Increase knowledge of the impact of psychosocial factors on the health of older adults.

3. Enhance skill in interdisciplinary teamwork in an outpatient health setting.

4. Increase knowledge of needs assessment and program evaluation.

ACTIVITIES

1. If you were one of the social workers hired to work on this project, describe the steps you would take to develop a working relationship with the physicians at your site.

2. Demonstrate through role-play how you would approach an elderly patient who has been referred to you for assessment of depression and/or cognitive impairment.

3. Given the stated goals of the project, what measures would you use to determine the effectiveness of this new pilot program?

4. Based on the experience of this project so far, what lessons have been learned about program implementation that would be useful if you were to start a new project, and that might help you avoid the problems encountered here?

SUGGESTED READINGS

Abramson, J., and Mizrahi, T. (1996). When social workers and physicians collaborate: Positive and negative interdisciplinary experiences. *Social Work, 41,* 270–280.

Keigher, S., Fortune, A., and Witkin, S. (2000). *Aging and social work: The changing landscapes.* Washington, DC: NASW Press.

Netting, F., and Williams, G. (1999). *Enhancing primary care of elderly people.* New York: Garland.

7-4   RESTORING ORGANIZATIONAL FUNCTIONING: CHALLENGE FOR A NEW EXECUTIVE DIRECTOR

Introduction

In many locales, master's level social workers move into administrative positions quickly. The case described here is somewhat typical of situations in which executive directors of social service agencies find themselves. Social workers may be called on to "fix" an organization in distress or that is struggling with growth and change. There are demands that require marshalling of many social work skills, including relationship building, group work, and community organization. Students apply principles of assessment to organizational problems and conflicts. The student can identify leadership issues and become aware of his or her own leadership style and abilities. Applicable frameworks are organizational theory, systems theory, and the problem-solving model.

Case Study

You have just been hired as executive director of a community-based health agency that provides comprehensive services to low-income clients. Centrally located, it is the only agency of its kind in this midsized city. The agency was set up fifteen years prior to your arrival and was well funded through federal and state health grants. The agency started as a small, intimate program with a cohesive staff that included the executive director, an associate director, one full-time physician who was the clinical director, one half-time physician, one full-time nurse, one full-time social worker, one health educator, a receptionist, and two clerical staff. The clinic occupied one floor of a shared building. There were two satellite centers that provided case management services, each having a half-time case manager, one in an African American neighborhood and another in a low-income multi-ethnic area. The agency was very community-oriented and had several users of the health center as board members. In addition, some users volunteered as health educators or to assist in the waiting room.

The staff grew to include an additional full-time social worker, a second full-time nurse, two additional half-time physicians, two case managers, two clerical staff, another receptionist, and a community outreach worker. One of the social workers became the director of social services. The clinic developed a collaborative relationship with a large teaching hospital in the city and participated in several research projects. The patient population doubled, and the agency outgrew its space. The agency started to look for a building that would house its expanded services.

About three years ago, the executive director, who was a nurse practitioner, retired, and a new executive was hired from the public sector. He had extensive experience as an administrator in the human services and was well known for his ability to manage a large budget, to bring in funds, and to get things done. Just as he was being hired, the agency acquired a building and everyone moved. Services were expanded further and now were delivered on two separate floors. All medical services were on one floor and all social services and administrative staff on another floor. The satellites were closed and moved into the centralized location. The agency was experiencing a variety of changes all at once: a new building, a new executive director, and an expanding staff that was no longer as close and informal.

The new executive director had a very different style. The first director had built the agency from the ground up, had hired all of the staff one by one, was very warm and nurturing, and had created considerable esprit de corps. She was very well liked in the community. The new director was somewhat distant from the staff, spent a great deal of time in his office, and was described by some as a "bureaucrat." He didn't have the personal relationships with staff that the first director had. The board was supportive of their new hire, as they believed that the agency was at a different stage and needed his budgetary and management skills. He began to consider ways to reorganize the services to make them more efficient and cost-effective. The professional staff who had worked hard over the years to make a comfortable environment for patients were resistant to change. They were used to a democratic decision-making process, and the senior staff had considerable authority over their areas of responsibility.

The director was frustrated at the staff's resistance and started to make changes without their acceptance. He cultivated staff who would support his program, and relationships between and among the senior staff became divisive and began to erode. Several senior staff described the situation as "intolerable" and resigned their positions over a ten-month period. Some staff who couldn't afford to leave stayed and simply toughed it out. Patients complained that the clinic was now impersonal and that they were processed in an assembly-line approach. The telephone system was automated, and it was difficult to get through to a person in a timely fashion. The African American community was dissatisfied that the case management services were moved and claimed that their community was no longer being served. Volunteers stopped providing services. The agency, in some sense, had a monopoly on community-based health services; therefore, alternatives were limited.

The board of the organization stuck by the director for eighteen months, hoping that the situation would stabilize and improve. However, even with new lead staff in place, there was considerable disharmony and continued complaints from the community. The board finally became extremely concerned, offered the director a severance package, and asked him to vacate the position. After a three-month search, you have been hired from the local community because of your administrative experience in the not-for-profit sector, your interdisciplinary experience, and your participatory leadership style.

LEARNING OBJECTIVES

1. Increase skill in assessment and analysis of a human service organization and enhance ability to discuss and defend the assessment coherently.

2. Apply administrative principles and knowledge of organizational dynamics to development of an administrative intervention plan.

3. Apply knowledge gained from work with individuals, families, and groups to organizational solutions.

ACTIVITIES

1. Using your understanding of organizational dynamics, what is your analysis of this situation? In your group, discuss your assessment and describe the problems/issues you believe need to be addressed.

2. Using a multilevel practice approach and using your knowledge of individuals and groups, discuss what you would do and list the order in which you would do it. Describe how you would check to make certain your efforts are being effective. Identify the theories and perspectives you are using to guide your work.

3. Discuss in your group the characteristics of an effective administrative leader. Choose an issue from the case and take turns demonstrating in your group how you would handle it as executive director.

4. How would you describe your own leadership style? Are there any areas you would like to develop further?

SUGGESTED READINGS

Anheier, H. (Ed.). (1999). *When things go wrong: Organizational failures and breakdowns.* Thousands Oaks, CA: Sage.

Harrison, M., and Shirom, A. (1999). *Organizational diagnosis and assessment: Bridging theory and practice.* Thousand Oaks, CA: Sage.

Herman, R., and Heimovics, R. (1991). *Executive leadership in nonprofit organizations.* San Francisco: Jossey-Bass.

Larson, C., and LaFasto, F. (1989). *Teamwork: What must go right/what can go wrong.* Newbury Park, CA: Sage.

Senge, P. (1996). Leading learning organizations. In *The leader of the future.* San Francisco: Jossey-Bass.

Stern, G. (1999). *The Drucker foundation self-assessment tool.* San Francisco: Jossey-Bass.

Wood, M. (1996). *Nonprofit boards and leadership.* San Francisco: Jossey-Bass.

CHAPTER EIGHT

FURTHER REFLECTIONS ON PROBLEM-BASED LEARNING AND THE CASE STUDY METHOD

The cases in this manual represent a small yet diverse sample of the types of situations faced by contemporary social workers. Case reporters selected cases that they believed were important and could impart knowledge that students might not otherwise encounter. Each case has many facets. I chose learning objectives and activities to cover a broad spectrum of knowledge, theories, and practice interventions. Others could be developed; therefore, students and faculty who use this manual are encouraged to add their own. Some instructors will want to use the cases in other ways to carry out their own teaching goals; others will appreciate the format and structure that is provided.

Case presentation and case analysis have always been part of social work practice and social work education. The inclusion of a full discussion of the problem-based method is intended to stimulate faculty who may or may not have used case studies in the past to think critically about the method and the various ways it can be implemented. It also provides an educational framework that makes the use of case studies more systematic.

This manual focuses on the use of written case studies. However, videotaped cases can also be used with a problem-based learning approach. Scenarios from the case studies can be videotaped by students in order to demonstrate responses to study questions. Or videotaped cases can be used as an alternative. Videotapes allow students to see visual representations of the study scenarios and to critique practice applications that are on tape. A stop-and-go method can be used in order to allow students to reflect on what is happening in the case at different stages with different amounts of information available to them. Written case studies can be revised into a Web-based interactive format. This method is particularly suited for individual self-guided learning, which could then be brought back to the group for shared learning. Finally, a very promising approach, which has been used in some social work programs and at some medical schools, is the use of simulated clients (Linsk and Tunney, 1997). The student social worker interacts with an actor client who dramatizes a case scenario. This is usually done behind a one-way mirror. After the enactment, students discuss the interaction either in the total class or in small groups. The simulation can also be videotaped for future use. This method has the benefit of closely approximating a live interaction.

CASE STUDIES ARE EDUCATIONAL AND RESEARCH TOOLS

Case development is a tool for learning for students and faculty. Faculty who are also in practice can use their own cases to illustrate certain learning objectives. There is also a rich pool of cases that students bring to the classroom from the field. Students can write them as case studies in order to learn from them and can then teach student colleagues what they have learned. With the permission of the student, an instructor can incorporate student case studies into the course for future use. Field instructors can also be involved in developing cases, thus giving them an amplified role in contributing to the educational process. I have found that case reporters were excited about telling their case stories and pleased at having their work included in the manual.

Guidelines for the creation of case studies, which both students and instructors can use, help to focus the case on evocative material and self-guided learning. Wasserman (1994, pp. 39–58) devotes a full chapter to the development of case studies and highlights several considerations in their design. Her recommendations include an opening paragraph that gets the reader interested and involved, ensuring that the case is credible, depicting issues and events that are important, and providing controversy or a dilemma that must be worked through or resolved. A thoughtful approach to developing study questions will be invaluable in maximizing learning from the case. A first line of inquiry would be to examine what is going on in the case from a descriptive point of view. A second level would be to develop an analysis of the events and issues. Thirdly, students delve more deeply into the issues, make evaluations, propose solutions, and apply this previously learned knowledge to the case, and apply this learned knowledge to other situations. The wording of questions is important, that is, they should stimulate critical thinking, invite rather than command explanations, and be clear rather than abstract or vague (Wasserman 1994, pp. 48–58). For example, opening words might be "In what ways," "What do you see as," or "How do you assess" rather than "Explain," "Justify," or words that lead to a "right" answer or "yes" or "no" response.

Problem-based learning has been referred to as a form of constructivist inquiry (Brown and King, 2000). Students are challenged to "make meaning" of the events in the case, which is based on a "real" or "authentic" situation. It is a ground-up learning experience. There may be no other examples quite like the case at hand; therefore, novel approaches or original ways of applying existing knowledge may be called for. The case may represent a watershed event in the field of social work; therefore, the case itself may contribute to new knowledge. In that sense, the collection and systematic analysis of case studies is a form of qualitative investigation (Odell, 2001). The case may provide a counterexample to conventional practice wisdom or to previously held theories about how to intervene in a particular situation. Cases, then, can be opportunities for theory building as well as to apply theories.

FURTHER RESEARCH ON USING THE CASE STUDY METHOD

Considerable research has been done on different aspects of PBL, yet still more can be done to acquire knowledge about student learning (Sykes, 1990, p. 301), on what makes groups effective in the learning process (Schwartz, Mennin, and Webb, 2001, p. 140), and on the instructor role. Who learns best with problem-based learning? In what situations do different variations of the method work best? Does PBL influence attitudes toward lifelong learning, toward curiosity and library use? Research on the transformative process from traditional learning to self-guided learning in students and from traditional teaching to the PBL method in faculty would be useful. Inquiry into how PBL impacts the use of the case study method in social work would also be enlightening.

Classroom research is an efficient way to gain feedback from students on methods and tools that are being tried. I have tested the use of case studies collected for this manual and then surveyed students about their experience. Since the students were in a learning environment where various approaches to learning were being used—including case studies, field instruction, lecture, readings, and various class assignments—students were asked about the relative importance of different aspects of their learning to see where case studies fit into the total picture. The importance of case studies in learning about micro and macro practice was also examined.

Classroom discussion and field placements were rated important by most students for learning about both social justice and clinical skills. More than two-thirds of the students rated the case studies as important or very important in learning both social justice and clinical skills. Classroom discussion, field experience, and required readings were most important in learning about social justice. Case studies were rated by more students as important in learning about clinical skills than in learning about social justice. Classroom discussion and field experience were equally important in learning about clinical skills; however, fewer students rated them so for learning about clinical skills than for learning about social justice.

More than ninety percent of the students "strongly agreed" or "agreed" that the cases allowed them to see how macro level issues affect individuals. The case study manual challenged and enhanced their critical thinking skills, and they found it to be a valuable tool in learning multilevel practice. Eighty-one percent said it was "very important" to "important" in enabling them to move back and forth between micro and macro issues. When asked about the importance of incorporating social justice into their social work practice in relation to other priorities, since coming to graduate school, eighty-four percent said it has "increased" or "somewhat increased."

The research did not investigate various aspects of problem-based learning that accompanied the use of the case studies. That would be a next line of inquiry. It did, however, indicate that case studies were important to their learning. Class assignments, reading, and discussion often relate to the case studies. Therefore, fine-tuning of the research questions could help sort out what is case study–related and what is not.

THE FUTURE OF PROBLEM-BASED LEARNING IN SOCIAL WORK EDUCATION

Problem-based learning is a promising approach for social work education, as it builds on and fits well with the tradition of using cases. The knowledge and experience that social workers have with learning and working in small groups also provides a good foundation. There are several aspects, however, that may require a cognitive shift for students and/or faculty. First is the change in the power relationship between the instructor and students, which gives more responsibility and control to students. Second is the priority given to self-guided learning, which may be a new experience for many students, who will require assistance in taking on this role. Third is the need to be disciplined and systematic in developing case material and the accompanying study questions. Fourth, the use of PBL may require some faculty to totally revamp their teaching style. And last is the need for constant scrutiny and evaluation of the entire process.

The question of whether it is desirable to have a total social work program based on PBL, as is the case with the Harvard Business School, requires further thought and study. Among the advocates for PBL there are different perspectives on exactly how it should be used, for example, whether didactic material should be presented before or after a case or at all. In the typical social work curriculum, any class, including those that sometimes have a strong lecture component such as social policy or human growth and behavior, could incorporate case studies. There may be benefits to having diverse approaches to teaching and learning within and among classes to respond to various student learning needs. It is not desirable to impose a particular method on all faculty, as it may not fit with their teaching abilities or style and could violate academic freedom. On the other hand, it is important to pay attention to research that shows certain approaches are more effective at producing objectives such as knowledge retention or commitment to lifelong learning. These issues are not yet settled.

Expansion of PBL program-wide would require faculty buy-in and faculty development to provide the necessary skills for successful implementation. As with any organizational change, this would require a carefully designed strategy in order to build consensus.

REFERENCES

Brown, S., and King, F. (2000). Constructivist pedagogy and how we learn: Educational psychology meets international studies. *International Studies Perspectives, 1,* 245–254.

Linsk, N., and Tunney, K. (1997). Learning to care: Use of practice simulation to train health social workers. *Journal of Social Work Education, 33,* 473–489.

Odell, J. (2001). Case study methods in international political economy. *International Studies Perspectives, 2,* 161–176.

Schwartz, P., Mennin, S., and Webb, G. (2001). *Problem-based learning: Case studies, experience, and practice.* London: Kogan Page.

Sykes, G. (1990). Learning to teach with cases. *Journal of Policy Analysis and Management, 9,* 297–302.

Wasserman, S. (1994). *Introduction to case method teaching.* New York: Teachers College Press.

GLOSSARY

Advanced generalist perspective: an integrated approach to social work practice that supports intervention at multiple levels—including individual, family, organizational, and community—using integrated theories to understand and to support interventions.

Attention-Deficit Hyperactivity Disorder: a persistent pattern of inattention and/or hyperactivity-impulsivity that is more frequent and severe than is typically observed in individuals at a comparable level of development.

Autism: a developmental disorder of brain function that includes three types of symptoms: impaired social interaction, problems with verbal and nonverbal communication and imagination, and unusual or severely limited activities and interests.

Case study method: a method of teaching and learning professional practice through the use of short vignettes or narratives drawn from the field that depict a situation or critical incident that students are likely to encounter and/or illustrate the application of a theory or theories and intervention modalities.

"Case" to "cause": the ability to move from client- or "micro-" focused interventions to population- or "macro-" focused activity based on an assessment that moving to another level will improve the effectiveness of response to multiple persons.

Clinical reasoning: the ability to think through a case problem or solution systematically—using knowledge, theory, research, and experience to inform the process.

Cognitive-behavioral approach: focuses on thinking, beliefs, interpretations, and images. Based on the theory that emotional reactions and maladaptive behavior are mediated by thoughts.

Combination drug therapies: treatment regimens for HIV and AIDS that utilize two or more drugs to respond to the HIV virus; sometimes known as cocktails.

Conflict resolution: a process of resolving differences or disputes based on cooperative, peaceful, and nonviolent means.

Constructivist perspective: a theoretical approach to persons and their environment that relies on the ways in which individuals and groups make meaning of a situation.

Cooperative learning: an approach to learning that utilizes small group processes, between and among students, to foster exchange of ideas, knowledge building, and practice competence.

Countertransference: any reaction of a social worker to the client on the cognitive, affective, physical, social, and spiritual dimensions and that may be rooted both in the past and the present.

Crisis intervention: a method of intervention, based on systems theory, that is a means of helping people under acute distress restore their psychosocial functioning to their precrisis level or to an improved level.

Differential diagnosis: the process of arriving at a client diagnosis using a systematic decision tree process.

Dual perspective in social work: the ability to understand client concerns and problems from the interpersonal perspective as well as the social justice aspect.

Ecosystems framework: a conceptual model that focuses on the interaction and reciprocity between the person and the environment.

Empowerment theory: a framework for understanding the power relationships between people and institutions that informs practice aimed at addressing inequality, social injustice, inadequate resources, and intolerance.

Evidence-based practice: social work practice that incorporates research into understanding personal, family, and social problems and that utilizes the most current research to make decisions about the most effective interventions.

Family systems theory: a framework for assessment and intervention with families that addresses the processes and interrelationships between and among family members, and the relationship between the family and its environment.

Feminist theory: an empowerment perspective that addresses gender-related inequalities and injustice, focusing on an individual or group's experience in its political and social context.

Human diversity: the range of differences in human beings that must be taken into account in social work practice, including age, ethnic/racial/cultural background, gender, sexual orientation, social class, family membership, occupational status, and health status.

Intersubjectivity: the belief that the human mind is interactive and that the therapeutic process should be understood as occurring between subjects rather than solely within the individual.

Mental status exam: an assessment tool to determine emotional and cognitive functioning including emotions, appearance, perceptual and thought disturbances, memory, orientation, judgment, insight, and impulse control.

Milieu therapy: therapeutic interventions delivered in an institutional environment as clients are engaged in daily living activities.

Multilevel practice: social work practice that includes both client-based (e.g., individual, family, group) and population-based assessment and interventions (e.g., organizational, community, global) in any case situation.

Narrative-based intervention: a theoretical perspective on social work practice based on constructivist theory that assists clients in constructing meaning out of experiences and events that may be otherwise incomprehensible through sharing and telling their story.

Oppositional Defiant Disorder: a pattern of angry, defiant, and disobedient behavior in youth toward those in authority that continues for at least six months.

Oppression theory: focuses on relationships between and among individuals, groups, classes, and societies; based on domination and exploitation as a source of economic, social, and psychological injustice.

Prevention: intervention to reduce the incidence, duration, and degree of impairment due to adverse conditions or events in clients or client populations.

Primary intervention attempts to reduce the rate of new cases of a disorder or condition.

Secondary intervention attempts to shorten duration of time in which individuals or populations experience problems (i.e., to prevent them from getting worse).

Tertiary intervention attempts to restore functioning to the highest level possible and prevent complications in individuals or populations experiencing a particular problem or condition.

Problem-based learning (PBL): an educational approach that uses problem situations or cases as vehicles for developing clinical reasoning, problem-solving skills, new knowledge, and self-guided learning.

Psychoanalytical approach: focuses on making changes in the personality structure through the use of unconscious material and client transference.

Resilience: the ability to bounce back or recover from a traumatic or adverse condition or event.

Risk and resilience perspective: the ability to handle adverse life conditions and events; it is related to a combination of risk and protective factors that reduce vulnerability and foster successful functioning. Interventions focus on reducing risk factors and enhancing protective factors.

Schizophrenia: a syndrome characterized by several types of symptoms including agitation, immobility, delusions, hallucinations, incoherent thoughts, and disorganized or withdrawn behavior.

Social interdependence: believed by some educators to be the fundamental ingredient for successful outcomes in models of group learning.

Solution-focused approach: a method of intervention that seeks to alleviate complaints or distress by assisting clients to search for exceptions to unwanted behavior, in order to seek change.

Strengths perspective: focuses on client capacities, abilities, and skills rather than on "deficits" or "pathology," and builds on them to strengthen clients' adaptation and coping mechanisms.

Task-centered social work: an approach to intervention based on short-term models that is characterized by highly specific tasks, sharp focus, and time limits.

Trauma perspective: focuses on traumatic events or stressors rather than individual difficulties as the problem to be addressed to restore coping abilities.

Witnessing trauma: listening to the testimony of a trauma survivor to allow the person to reconstruct the story as a part of the process of healing.

INDEX